Insight and On Site

Insight and On Site

The Architecture of Diamond and Schmitt

A.J. Diamond, Donald Schmitt and Don Gillmor

Douglas & McIntyre Ltd.

2323 Quebec Street, Suite 201

Vancouver, British Columbia

Canada V5T 4S7

www.douglas-mcintyre.com

Library and Archives Canada Cataloguing in Publication

Gillmor, Don

   Insight and On Site : The Architecture of Diamond and Schmitt /
Don Gillmor.

ISBN 978-1-55365-277-9

      1. Diamond and Schmitt Architects. 2. Architecture, Modern–21st
century. 3. Sustainable architecture. I. Title.

NA749.D52G54 2008   720.92'271   C2008-900426-4

Jacket photograph by Tim Griffith.

Design by Wonder inc.

Printed and bound in Canada by Friesens.

Printed on acid-free paper.

We gratefully acknowledge the financial support of the Canada Council
for the Arts, the British Columbia Arts Council, the Province of British
Columbia through the Book Publishing Tax Credit, and the Government
of Canada through the Book Publishing Industry Development Program
(BPIDP) for our publishing activities.

Acknowledgements 8
Foreword by Richard Florida 9

The Principals of Diamond and Schmitt Architects in conversation
with Witold Rybczynski 11

There Is a There There: The Context of Design 24

- 30 Jerusalem City Hall, Jerusalem, Israel
- 36 Marion McCain Faculty of Arts and Social Sciences Building,
  Dalhousie University, Halifax, Nova Scotia
- 38 Bank Street Building Competition, Parliament Hill, Ottawa, Ontario
- 42 The Jewish Community Center in Manhattan, New York, New York
- 48 Gerstein Science Information Centre – Master Plan and Renovations,
  University of Toronto, Toronto, Ontario
- 56 The Banff Centre – Campus Master Plan and Implementation, Banff, Alberta

The Individual to the Collective: Shaping the City 60

- 66 East Bayfront Master Plan Proposal, Toronto, Ontario
- 68 TEDCO's Corus Building, Toronto, Ontario
- 70 Los Alamos Civic Center, Los Alamos, New Mexico
- 74 Urban Block Redevelopment, Regent Park, Toronto, Ontario

All Together Now: The Compact City 76

- 82 Sidney Harman Hall, Washington, District of Columbia
- 88 Li Ka Shing Knowledge Institute, St. Michael's Hospital, Toronto, Ontario
- 90 The Hudson Condominiums, Toronto, Ontario
- 92 Ways Lane, Toronto, Ontario
- 94 Charlie Condominiums, Toronto, Ontario
- 95 Minto Lonsdale Condominiums, Toronto, Ontario
- 96 Life Sciences Complex, McGill University, Montreal, Quebec

An Inner Order: Beauty Is More than Skin Deep 98

- 104 The Esplanade Arts and Heritage Centre, Medicine Hat, Alberta
- 108 Richmond Hill Central Library, Richmond Hill, Ontario
- 112 Integrated Sciences Building, Drexel University, Philadelphia, Pennsylvania
- 116 Cambridge City Hall, Cambridge, Ontario
- 118 Student Centre, York University, Toronto, Ontario

Parts and Parcels: The Elements of Architecture 120

126 Alumbrera House, Mustique, The Grenadines
130 Leggatt Hall and Watts Hall, Queen's University, Kingston, Ontario
134 Metro Central YMCA, Toronto, Ontario
138 College Residences, Lakeshore Campus and North Campus, Humber College, Toronto, Ontario
142 Maria Shchuka District Branch Library, Toronto, Ontario
144 Southbrook Vineyards, Niagara-on-the-Lake, Ontario
146 Medical Education Building, University of Windsor, Windsor, Ontario

Illumination and Movement: Architecture as Kinetic Art 148

152 The Israeli Ministry of Foreign Affairs, Jerusalem, Israel
162 The Apotex Centre, Toronto, Ontario
166 Pierre Berton Resource Library, Vaughan, Ontario
172 Ontario Science Centre – Master Plan and Renovations, Toronto, Ontario
178 Holy Blossom Temple, Toronto, Ontario
180 Susur Restaurant, Toronto, Ontario

Intelligent Design: Towards a Sustainable World 182

188 University of Ontario Institute of Technology – Campus and Buildings, Oshawa, Ontario
196 University of Guelph-Humber, Toronto, Ontario
200 Evergreen at the Brick Works, Toronto, Ontario
202 Centre for Advanced Manufacturing and Design Technologies, Sheridan College, Brampton, Ontario
206 Life Sciences Centre, University of British Columbia, Vancouver, British Columbia
212 Indigo Residence, Mustique, The Grenadines

Life in Old Structures: Renovation and Reuse 214

220 Betty Oliphant Theatre, National Ballet School, Toronto, Ontario
222 Capital Information Centre, Ottawa, Ontario
224 Canadian Chancery, Prague, Czech Republic
226 Berkeley Castle, Toronto, Ontario
228 Legislative Assembly of Ontario – Renovation Master Plan and Implementation, Toronto, Ontario

Waste Not: Economy of Means 232

238 Regent Park Community Health Centre, Toronto, Ontario
242 Cawthra Community Centre, Mississauga, Ontario
246 Memorial Pool, Toronto, Ontario
248 Davenport Wing, Lash Miller Chemistry Building,
    University of Toronto, Toronto, Ontario
250 Thayer Building, University of Michigan, Ann Arbor, Michigan

Not by Bread Alone: Building for the Arts 252

256 Four Seasons Centre for the Performing Arts, Toronto, Ontario
266 Garter Lane Arts Centre, Waterford, Ireland
268 Max M. Fisher Music Center, Detroit, Michigan
274 Agnes Etherington Art Centre, Queen's University, Kingston, Ontario
276 New Brunswick Museum, Saint John, New Brunswick
278 Country Day School Performing Arts Centre, King City, Ontario

A Lesson in Building: Spaces for Education 280

286 Academic Library, University of Ontario Institute of Technology, Oshawa, Ontario
294 Computer Science and Engineering Building, University of Michigan,
    Ann Arbor, Michigan
300 Campus Master Plan, McGill University, Montreal, Quebec
302 Anthony P. Toldo Health Education Centre, University of Windsor,
    Windsor, Ontario
304 School of Image Arts, Ryerson University, Toronto, Ontario
306 Earth Sciences Centre, University of Toronto, Toronto, Ontario
308 School of Computer Science and Engineering,
    The Hebrew University of Jerusalem, Jerusalem, Israel
310 Bahen Centre for Information Technology, University of Toronto, Toronto, Ontario

PROJECT LIST 322

STAFF LIST 330

THE FIRM 331

BIOGRAPHIES 332

AWARDS 338

SELECT BIBLIOGRAPHY 341

INDEX 344

ACKNOWLEDGEMENTS

This book is dedicated to the members of Diamond and Schmitt, past and present, whose talent, dedication and enthusiasm have made the works illustrated in this book possible.

As the dedication notes, this book represents the contribution of many whose names do not appear on these pages, but to whom we are greatly indebted.

Special note, however, is given to those who, in addition to their normal (if that word can be used for their extraordinary but usual efforts) work in the firm, helped produce this book: Elizabeth Gyde, whose discerning eye and quiet efficiency elevate the quality of the visual representation of our work; Robb Graham, whose energy and judgment separate the deserving content from the dross; Nisha Lewis, who brings experience and control to our unruly narratives; Martin Davidson and Michael Leckman, whose intervention in the early discussions on the substance of the book gave fresh insights and varied perspectives to the discourse.

Without Sara Angel's patience with, and management of, the enterprise, this book would probably have been published posthumously. We were fortunate to have the excellent writing skills of Don Gillmor at our disposal and were blessed with the choice of Anita Matusevics and Jason Halter as the designers of the book. Editors are essential, even for the most skilled authors. In the case of architects this is an indispensable function, to translate grammarless jargon into understandable English. This task was miraculously performed by Rosemary Shipton and Patricia Holtz, with the assistance of Amy Hick and Marta Braun. Special thanks, as well, go to Doug Laxdal and Jeff Hale at The Gas Company for their expertise in the production of the scans and proofs of the images used in the book.

Not least are the accolades which must go to our estimable publisher, Scott McIntyre. He is a generous, understanding and, in our case, long suffering, publisher of the highest standard. We are proud to be associated with a Canadian publishing company that stands so tall – in any company.

A.J. Diamond and Donald Schmitt
June 2008

Little houses on a hillside, little houses made of ticky-tacky. It's a song that belches out of my TV set – the big flat thing on the wall – the theme for a program called *Weeds.* We are surrounded not only by what Jim Kunstler calls the geography of nowhere but an architecture of meaninglessness – strip malls, big box stores and so much generic, so much all the same.

Against the backdrop of such mundanity, is it any wonder that we have seen such a surge in an architecture of extravagance, of spectacle, of statement? The celebrity architect. The celebrity building. Just call it "iconic" – it won't sound quite so gauche. But is it really all that different than Britney Spears or Donald Trump?

Insight and On Site by A.J. Diamond, Donald Schmitt and Don Gillmor, gives us a manifesto for a new, more sensitive architecture. Not in a touchy-feely, let's-all-hold-hands-and-sing-Kumbaya way, but in a way that emphasizes context, sustainability, community and creativity. And in so doing, they go a long way toward reining in the cult of celebrity in architecture and the built environment. As they see it, architecture is neither a thing-in-itself nor an end-in-itself. It functions best – or perhaps it only really functions – when part of an organic, vital, human community. As I read it, their work is organized around four key principles, which, when taken together, suggest nothing less than a new paradigm for a humbler and better architecture of the city.

One, context yourself. To paraphrase those great 1970s philosophers, Humble Pie: *I don't need no iconic buildings.* Architecture that stands up and screams at you, *look at me, look at me,* is something we all need to get beyond. The best buildings, like the best cities, are inviting and exciting; they pull you with subtlety and nuance.

Two, you only get what you need. For too long, architecture has been about splendour and spectacle – and waste. But today the best cities, like the best companies and certainly the best buildings, are creatures of limits. Diamond and Schmitt call this an *economy of means.* Truly great architecture does not arrogantly squander scarce resources. Why use any more materials than necessary, in an era where profligacy is decimating our resources and leaving the planet depleted for future generations?

Three, dialectic is always enlightenment. We've all heard the debates about form and function – old news. Or maybe new again. Truly great architecture is shaped by the constant push and pull of the internal and the external. Who wants to live in a monument with empty rooms and no furniture, after all? On the inside, the best buildings envelop and energize their inhabitants and users. On the outside, they fit seamlessly into their community context – improving, enticing and energizing the community without overpowering it.

Four, stewards of the *we.* Architects have an additional obligation – as stewards of urban space and the public realm. Great buildings give us something bigger than ourselves, something that can fill the soul, something that we can pass down from generation to generation. Can we have an architecture in and of the public interest?

Diamond and Schmitt draw a line in the sand. They challenge us to provide an architecture that will uplift and inspire, strengthen and connect and never, ever overpower. They call upon us to build connected, inclusive, sustainable and creative communities. Most of all, in a time of great turmoil, they give us hope that architecture can fit into and help uncover the true soul of the city.

Richard Florida
Toronto 2008

Interview of the fourteen principals of Diamond and Schmitt Architects, conducted by writer and architecture critic Witold Rybczynski, February 28, 2008

Witold Rybczynski: Let's first talk about making a virtue of necessity, which seems to be a theme in your work.

DSAI: The obvious historical example is the cathedral. In order to lighten the heavy walls and reduce the amount of stone, the wall was propped up with a buttress. Then the buttress became celebrated and it evolved into an elegant piece of architecture. The rose window was used to lighten the wall once again, and it too became celebrated. There was no arbitrariness to it. Its virtue lay in its function. So that's making a virtue of a necessity. Making virtues of necessities has to do with designing from first principles, designing relative to the program. Architects sometimes make the mistake of bringing preconceptions to a project, whether it's stylistic preoccupations or a preconceived idea of the institution.

A more ideological approach?

Yes, an ideological approach. Amateurs and ideologues are essentially the same. An amateur has a vision of a house he wants to build; perhaps that vision is a chateau. Then he or she buys land in the Caribbean and that's what they build there, despite the lack of cultural or practical context. The amateur has a picture in his mind, a picture from a magazine, and he won't budge from it.

Ideologues are the same. Regardless of the circumstances, they bring their ideology to it. Their instincts about shape and form are imposed on the project. We design from the inside out. It means spending time determining what the functional demands of a particular project are. You need to understand the attitudes and goals and culture of the institution, and then find an architecture that evolves from the necessities of the program.

A great deal of our time is spent on the schematic design phase, sorting out the arrangement of all the programmatic elements. That's where the opportunities emerge, opportunities to provide things that aren't written in the text of the program itself, to create something that is more than just the sum of the programmatic parts. Making virtues out of necessities is the meshing of the client's needs with what the architect is bringing to the project. The Gothic example is a good one. The builders loved those pointed arches. There was absolutely no structural logic to it, they just liked the shape. It was exotic and new. So they were meeting the needs of the program, but they were also bringing something else to it, which was their fascination with that geometric shape.

There is a theory that sometimes, when an institution builds a monumental building, it's a sign that the institution is in trouble. For example, St. Peter's in Rome was built at the nadir of the Catholic Church. Only four years after the AT&T building in New York, designed by Philip Johnson, was built the corporation was broken up thanks to an antitrust ruling.
It's an interesting theory, the idea that an excessive building can be an indication of the decay of the institution. We look to create buildings that quietly achieve a noble and lofty objective. They aren't advertisements, and they don't consume the kind of resources that can compromise the institution.

Is the so-called iconic building a reasonable vehicle to meet a client's needs?
The iconic building raises the question of what drives a career. It's like the couturiers who do something outrageous in order to get recognition. Iconic buildings speak to real estate issues. They provide instant recognition and it makes the buildings easier to lease. It's

easy to do an iconic building, because it's only solving one issue. It's not resolving a complex set of issues. It's like building an expressway through a neighbourhood. You get the cars through quickly, but all the myriad outfall of that solution – of what happens to the residential area, what happens at either end when you have to park the car – all that is ignored. There are times when you need a building that has iconic status, when it's justified by the institution itself. It's justified by the location in the city, and by its importance in society. But most of the time it's not driven by those inherent requirements, it's driven by external factors like career or real estate or ego. And that's a conflict, and the difficult thing is to resist that.

The competition process plays into it, too. So much of it is a beauty contest, and the trend toward iconic buildings is having a significant impact on the outcome of competitions. There is a drive for the extraordinary and the extravagant, the avant-garde. You have to get the attention of the jury in fifteen minutes.

There are so many forces that work toward compressing what we do. So much of what we fight against is the immediate eye-grabbing vision of the building, as opposed to a more considered understanding of the building's program. We're looking at the long term. Few people consider the overall timeline of the building, of where it fits in history.

Quite often the reason we get beautiful looking but bad buildings is that they're really not based upon the experiential aspect of the building or the resolution of the problems within it; they're based upon a graphic. You can make buildings that are graphically gorgeous, but a graphic design that has great beauty can translate into a building that is pretty sterile.

But does that mean they're mutually exclusive?
No. But graphics should be a means to an end in architecture, not an end in itself.

Renzo Piano has been quoted as saying that the problem with the computer in architecture is that it speeds up the design process, so you can have a baby in nine weeks instead of nine months—but you still really need nine months. I wonder what role the computer plays in your practice.

A design takes a while to evolve. It just requires time to cook. And sometimes you can tell someone has drawn something on a computer and it doesn't look like it's fully resolved, but it's looking very finished. The computer gives an authority to a set of ideas that is out of sync with the level of resolution. It gives legitimacy at a much earlier stage.

The issue here is about conceptualization and what is the best tool to conceptualize design. Drawing by hand is a bit like seeing faces in clouds. As you draw, you see new things. The computer doesn't allow for that imprecision. It's a wonderful tool to represent an idea or to help visualize an idea that has already been determined, to get a sense of it spatially.

I look at architecture today and I see two schools of design. There are those designing buildings that could not be produced without computers, and there are those whose buildings don't rely on computers at all. Your firm seems to be firmly situated in that second school...

We're the first school. The other's the second school.

I think the strength of this practice is that we are in both camps, yet what you observe is the strength of the tradition. Architects have aspired to build very complex buildings for a long time. The stadium in Beijing and all those very complex geometries that come with plastically molded buildings really are computer driven. It would take eons to draw out by hand, if you had to do it.

The young Turks want computers to create buildings on their own. They write algorithms that automatically produce different forms.
There's the ability now to realize whatever your brain or an algorithm can imagine. There's the ability to produce realistic renderings that look like you're standing in front of the real building or walk you through a building where you can see the design long before any of it exists. The computer has so many applications, and one has to be judicious about how they are used.

It comes back to what you think architecture should be about. Here's an analogy in the contemporary art field. At a recent exhibition, one of the exhibits was bread that was growing mould. It was simply slices of bread, and the artistic experience was to watch the bread change, to observe the forms and colour of its mould. So the effect isn't determined by the artist. It's an artifact that's determined by the phenomenon of its existence and by change. And I think that the architectural equivalent of this is the algorithm. It's got nothing to do with function, it's got nothing to do with the rational aspects of the life of the building. It has to do with the artistic aspect. And the sensibility about architecture now is that it's architecture for art's sake.

Not all art movements develop into something significant. They can come to a dead end. The Dadaists protested what they felt was the conformity of conventional art, but their own expression was cynical and, ultimately, sterile. Architecture, by definition, isn't art in that sense. Some of the icon builders are using architecture to make a large art object. Whereas we see art as a way of enhancing the building designed around the judgments that we've been talking about, where the art is in the service of something. There are specific functions and responsibilities with buildings, whether it is a laboratory or a museum or a hospital or a house. Ultimately, you have to occupy the building. These people who are designing with the algorithm or the artist who's putting a cow in formaldehyde, they've taken out some of the human element and simply created an artifact.

Can we move on to the form of all those computer-generated buildings? Because ultimately they're an…
Accident.

I'm not sure they're not really accidental, because I see a very consistent set of forms: organic forms, crystalline forms, ruptured forms. The computer is just another means of producing a design.
It's form for form's sake, though. It has less to do with architecture than with fashion.

It comes back to the Gothic arch. As you said, the pointed arch wasn't really about structure, it was about a change in visual taste. I've come to believe that, in architecture, taste has enormous importance.
Sensibilities change, certainly. But when you use that extraordinary technology as a means and not an end, then it's in service to something that you've thought through conceptually and used your judgment on. Whereas, if it's simply the demonstration of how exceptional and extraordinary you can be, if that's the point of it, it's not a worthwhile point. In some ways, the computer is like giving a child an AK-47. It's too powerful – and they can do anything with it. And just because you can do it, doesn't mean you should do it.

I'm also skeptical that the computer is having a positive impact on architectural design, but there are precedents – the discovery of perspective, for instance, and how it inspired architects during the Renaissance.
It has certainly taken hold of the public consciousness. Is it the Gothic arch of today? The issue is how it is used, and it comes back to the iterative approach that we go through in design, which assumes a spirit of collaboration with the client. It's not just imposing ideas; it's the opportunity for the client to be involved, as well.

Let's move on to that subject. Architects always talk about the importance of the client. What makes a good client?

The beginning of a good client is having one whose values are similar. They may not understand architecture or what you do, but they have a set of values that are simpatico. That's one aspect of it. The other aspect is that while they will be demanding about what they want, they'll also be respectful about the way in which you accomplish it. There are clients who think they should be holding the pencil and that you're just a cipher, or a service that will draft and implement the technical aspects of a project. What's lost in that circumstance is an opportunity for discovery and collaboration.

There is no question that a good clients make a good building, and an engaged, even demanding client is an important part of the process.

It also requires courage on the part of the client. Some have an extremely limited view about what's possible, and you can expose them to a much broader and more ambitious scheme in order to satisfy their requirements, but they may not have the courage to go there. The architect can bring a vision to it, if there's a well-stated problem. And you can help them state the problem. Our clients are not always individuals with a singular view. They can be committees, or boards, or large groups of people who may not all have the same ideas about the project. They are stewards for public money and they often have different criteria than a private client might. Their immediate concern is usually: Is this going to come in on time and on budget? The challenge is to get them to look ten years out, or twenty years out. To ask the question, What is the legacy of this project? One of the challenges is to find out what constitutes success for a particular client. There are clients whose idea of success is simply to get major press coverage. There are others who are after longer term goals, and there are others who simply want the building to have low operating and maintenance costs. It's an interesting thing to discuss with clients: What do you think success is for this project?

And there are lots of levels of success – the operational end, design recognition, the fundraising component. We've had experiences where part of the client is not working toward the good of the building and the life of the building. We love librarians, because they live in the building. They know the intimate life in its truest sense and the necessity of a building is the life of the building. It's not simply the sum of a washroom and a stack and a corridor. The key is to align the vision and the people who control the purse strings.

I think the way the building is built is a big concern for you. Your buildings express how they're put together. So construction becomes part of the character of the building.

We are interested in the way buildings are made and we are interested in making them durable. Generally, there is a lightness in our buildings, both in the sense of the building as object, but also in our concern for natural light. That concern very much permeates the work. We see light as an essential quality of space, and we try and deal with it in the best manner in terms of the content and the context of the project.

This interest in construction differentiates your work from the classic modernism of someone like I.M. Pei, because Pei generally hides how his buildings are built, making his work appear more minimalist.

I think part of it has to do with the fact we work in Toronto, a town that knows how to make concrete and concrete buildings. There's a weight and authenticity that expresses the structure and it delineates the space. We've grown out of a tradition here of being able to use concrete. The choices in materials and their straightforward expression in the building is something that has informed our work.

What is it that makes your buildings look the way they do? Is there a signature look, or do they look different as the result of different situations?

Robert Venturi warned against "the easy unity of exclusion." Our philosophy is one of inclusiveness, where the buildings essentially narrate the content. Another key characteristic of our work is a preoccupation with the architectural promenade – the stairs and routes through buildings. Within complex programs, finding clarity for the public realm in a building – stairs, corridors, halls, courts – is very much a preoccupation. In terms of the envelope, its expression, there is an increasing preoccupation with solidity, in substantial contrast to transparency. A kind of ethereal minimalism that tries to dematerialize the screens between indoor and out. The envelope isn't done for its own sake but as a way to appropriately enclose the functions. It's the play of the solid and void, not just as a material thing but as a volumetric thing. So that you get transparent voids and transparent volumes and you get opaque volumes, and we play with them depending upon the levels of privacy required.

The composer Karlheinz Stockhausen has talked about the contrast between the individual and the "dividual," a word he invented. His theory is that the apex of art has to do with the artist resolving two conflicting and opposing ideas. And what are the two polar opposites in architecture? It's the defined volume, because we're dealing in space, that's our medium, and it's the deliberately destructive volume. To resolve those is to approach architecture at its most elevated.

Is there a sense of architectural coherence that is consistent across different projects?

Our buildings vary hugely in their expression, but the principles are consistent. There's an excitement to that, but it's not looking to express that excitement in a very busy way. There is still that simplification happening at the same time.

There are certain common themes throughout the work. The integrity of the materials that we use, for example. You won't see many buildings of ours where we've painted the wood. Usually, it's left in its natural state. So there is an authenticity, a calming vocabulary, if you like. There are plans coming out of this office that are essentially Beaux-Arts ordered, they have a symmetry that is deeply rooted in architectural history in a classical sense. At the same time, there's another group of buildings that have plans that are more expressive and looser in their configuration, even though the order in those spaces that are pinwheeling around the common form might be quite controlled.

Another characteristic of our work is a preoccupation with the way the building engages the landscape or the street. We tend to see institutional buildings as essentially a continuation and support of the public realm of the city. Addressing the public space of the interior and then negotiating the threshold between it and the street is an ongoing challenge.

Context is important in your work. There are a lot of parallels with someone like Piano, in terms of a modern style that isn't absolutely minimal and is a bit flexible, but context seems to play a bigger role in your work than it does in his.

For us context is fundamentally important – in opposition to the iconic building, which ignores or refutes its context. Contextualism, whether it's the immediate one of shaping outdoor spaces in relationship to the city or the larger political and social context, characterizes our work.

How does that express itself in terms of the appearance of the building?

There isn't a single orthodoxy or approach. Whether it's in terms of the selection of materials, the configuration of space or the way in which entrances are dealt with, there's not a single way to do it.

The contextual issues for us have always been about how things fit, politically, socially, physically, climatically. There is an apocryphal story about Mies van der Rohe explaining how to design a building in the Arctic and how he would design a building in the Sahara.

For both, his answer was, "With glass and steel." His buildings are elegant, but there is a regionalism in architecture; it's a legitimate force. And those contextual questions are very Canadian and very Toronto. And we're part of that school.

I've always thought that concern with the weather is a trait of Canadian architecture.

There's the practical issue of how buildings weather, given the climatic extremes. So the envelope and how one handles that envelope and how one deals with the harshness of the weather is also characteristic of our work.

Do buildings have an inherent social responsibility?

The social dimension is sometimes ignored by architects, and it's something we have to address. On the one hand, the world is becoming more and more isolated. Children are becoming socially inept, because they spend their time in front of the computer and don't deal with people. But that trend toward isolationist behaviors is coincident with the notion of convergence. You see it in universities and hospitals, where there is greater interaction between disciplines.

The social aspect of our buildings stems from the work that started the firm, the kind of urban exercises that were initially undertaken – how a building sits in its context and what it means for the surrounding neighbourhood or community. If it's an academic institution, then we look at how the interaction will take place among various disciplines, both in the formal work environment and in the informal public spaces.

One of the things we intuitively understand about architecture is its power to transform the institution. A great building will absolutely transform the institution and facilitate its institutional life. It will change it in dramatic, powerful ways. It's very hard to define that dimension. How can you measure the transformative capability of a building? But it is something we are very aware of. It's something we work toward.

How has the architecture of the firm changed over the years?

The scale of the buildings has changed, but our approach hasn't. The firm has always been innovative and continues to be. The green wall at Humber-Guelph was an important innovation. The University of Guelph was investigating the use of plants in closed environments such as the International Space Station.

Out of that came the bio-filter wall of living plants, which was designed to cleanse the air, and we've now applied it to several buildings. The air is drawn through the green wall, and it's purified by the natural biological processes and the toxicity is eliminated. I think we may be the first architects to have done this.

How would you characterize the current profile of your practice?
We're still very much a teaching office. When we all started, we always thought of it that way. When we bring new people into the firm, we're looking for people who have new interests and engagements; there is always a push toward fresh ideas and innovation. As a result, we've developed a lot of expertise in a lot of areas.

The famous architect has become a stereotype, both a literary stereotype – think of Ayn Rand's *The Fountainhead* – and increasingly, these days, a media stereotype. How do you see the role of fame in architecture?

Everybody is famous now. Once upon a time there were masters of architecture and they were few, and now everybody's a master. The idea of celebrity permeates the culture, the idea that everybody can be great, or at least famous. Everybody has to be a master. There are no masters anymore because everybody's one.

There Is a There There: The Context of Design

Celebrity is an increasingly valuable commodity — achievement is being supplanted by recognition.

Celebrity is an increasingly valuable commodity these days. It is by nature ephemeral, arriving suddenly and disappearing without explanation. Celebrity architecture is not a new development, but there is a danger that achievement is being supplanted by recognition. There is a trend towards iconic and singular public buildings that purposefully stand out. The praise for these works is largely aesthetic – they represent architecture as art, and the hope is that their forms will bring beauty to the skyline and favourable attention to the city.

In the hands of talented artists such as Bernini or Gaudi, this promise has often been borne out. Certainly, artistry is a component of great architecture. But the architecture-as-art philosophy has its drawbacks. Its foundations are purely aesthetic, and its buildings are prey to some of the vagaries of the art world. There are artists who wonderfully express their times. Andy Warhol's iconic celebrity portraits, for example, captured a moment in American culture. Eventually Warhol began painting portraits of lesser celebrities who paid $25,000 for the same treatment (and $5,000 for additional prints). Record executives, obscure royalty, and in the end the wives of Long Island dentists joined the queue. What began as art essentially became a commercial enterprise that owed as much to the assembly line as to art. In his lifetime, Warhol worried that his work lacked the depth of works by Jasper Johns and Robert Motherwell.

A building that brilliantly captures one moment often fails to capture the next. The architecture of many worlds' fairs, Albert Speers' Nazi architecture and postmodernism are all examples. Art can afford to deal in moments, but architecture has a longer timeline and a responsibility to society at large; it shapes the civic mood. When a building's aesthetic has become passé, when its unique shape degenerates into novelty, when its materials suddenly seem shabby and faded, it is judged on its usefulness rather than its beauty. Art doesn't need to be useful. It thrives in its role as critic, antagonist or provocateur. But there is a collectivity in architecture. Buildings are part of society, and they embody its laws, wealth, culture and history, as well as its art. They are rooted in the physical landscape, and they have to deal with the realities of climate and topography.

In the hands of a brilliant architect, the result of idiosyncratic, noncontextual design can be transcendent – Frank Gehry's Disney Hall in Los Angeles and Frank Lloyd Wright's Guggenheim Museum in New York being two examples. But as a school, iconic architecture is essentially solipsistic. It is more effective at building careers than cities.

There are a number of reasons why architects favour idiosyncratic design that ignores or spurns context. One of them is the context itself. The surrounding buildings may be diverse and homely, and understandably there is little desire for any association with them. And context isn't always easy to define. In a city such as Paris, it is gloriously obvious; the consistency of Baron Haussmann's plan defines the urban landscape. One of the reasons that Renzo Piano and Richard Rogers' iconic Centre Pompidou works so brilliantly is that it has Haussmann's consistent context to play against. The strength of the Parisian urban fabric allows for – even cries out for – some deviation.

But most North American cities don't have that consistency. They are a patchwork quilt of styles, eras, zoning laws and building types. Urban neighbourhoods often contain houses, apartment blocks and the shells of light industrial buildings. If a building's site is surrounded by empty lots and diverse structures, how is context defined? An iconic approach might exacerbate unfortunate civic truths: The surrounding structures are architecturally indifferent and poorly sited. But design can also be a way to make sense of existing buildings. This is the case with the Bahen Centre for Information Technology at the University of Toronto, the Jerusalem City Hall and the theatre at Toronto's National Ballet School. They attempt to create a dialogue, to preserve what is best while still embracing new technologies and fresh ideas. The way new buildings are organized, the connections they make, the exterior spaces they shape and the interior places they create – all these facets help to create a community.

The concept of community is of increasing concern in urban America. In his book *Bowling Alone: The Collapse and Revival of*

Sports Palace, Berlin: The architectural hubris of Albert Speer – an expression of German ultranationalism.

26

Apartments by Gaudi, Barcelona: Both icon and urban increment – the perfect resolution of opposing forces.

American Community, Harvard professor Robert Putnam wrote of the civic disengagement that plagues American cities. The same can be seen in Canadian cities. Voter turnout is low (Ontario's 2007 election had a historic low of 52.7 per cent), shared cultural references are shaky (63 per cent of Canadians can't cite the first line of the national anthem), there is growing isolation in some suburbs, a decline in social organizations and a rise in the use of social services. Design has a role in the building of communities, in making connections.

Context is critical because the public innately wants to make sense of architecture. People seek a connection to the buildings that surround them; they want a narrative. And now narrative has been seized as a marketing tool, a way to sell the building. Metaphors are attached as an afterthought, linking the structure to a neighbouring landmark, a historical feature or a cultural sensibility. At its crudest, this is the architectural equivalent of rock bands telling the audience how great it is to be in Toronto/Denver/ Edmonton. The architecture may exist solely for itself, but *ex post facto* attempts are made to have it fit into an identifiable history. We are comforted by stories.

The modern movement ignored context, but revolutions need to kill what came before. Attention to context needn't be imitative or rote. Replications rarely succeed; hundreds of awkward neo-Victorian houses attest to that. But a reinterpretation that respects physical, cultural, historic and architectural connections can help bring coherence to a site without sacrificing individuality.

Several forces support the current boom in iconic buildings. Commercial interests want something dramatic to sell. Museum directors and their boards want celebrated designs that will help raise money and draw press coverage for their institution. There

Andy Warhol, 1980. Warhol prints' fifteen minutes of fame – a sight bite.

are, as well, the fragile egos of provincial cities, which feel that a distinctive public building will confer envy and status. The corporate world occasionally seeks the biggest or the loudest structure as a declaration of market share, an advertisement. Architectural journals also contribute to the trend towards architectural gigantism. Many want striking images on their covers – the more idiosyncratic, the better.

These buildings will be judged on their individual merits. Some will have lasting drama, and others will be the equivalent of teen celebrities that showed early promise but ultimately lacked depth. But they will all be with us for decades, and the city will have no choice but to accommodate their idiosyncrasies and tantrums.

Beauty is a noble ideal, but we shouldn't be seduced by every unique silhouette that appears on the skyline. There is a beauty in the way a building can tease new meaning from its context, satisfy the needs of its constituency and embrace the values and character of its community. Architecture shouldn't lose track of the larger issues: the existing cityscape, practicality, sustainability and adaptability. We should be wary of the architectural equivalent of the thirty-second sound bite – the sight bite.

The Earth Sciences Centre at the University of Toronto shapes public space, creates campus paths and engages history.

Watercolour of the Temple Mount in Jerusalem.

JERUSALEM CITY HALL, JERUSALEM, ISRAEL

Before the Industrial Revolution, buildings reflected the locale, materials and limited technology of their day, and all these restrictions on structures imparted a consistent texture and scale to cities. To maintain this conformity in the hallowed city of Jerusalem, the British Mandate ruled after the First World War that all new buildings were to be constructed, or at least faced, with local limestone, known as Jerusalem stone. This ochre and salmon stone is beautiful, and, as finished by Arab stone masons, it has a rich variety of textures.

Mamelukes, then Turks, used light grillework in metal or wood that gave a delicacy to the monolithic character of the stone. This contrast was highlighted by painting the grillework in blue, and sometimes adding blue tile in special structures such as the Dome of the Rock. Mamelukes also employed another subtle scaling device – alternating bands of masonry in ochre- and salmon-coloured stone. The City Hall is a contemporary expression of all these historic devices.

The spaces between the buildings provide cohesive links between the main plaza and the surrounding areas. There is a dramatic contrast between the formality of the plaza, where programmed activities are staged, and the more intimate informal gardens and cafés. To unite the structures and tie them to the city, all the buildings are faced with Jerusalem stone.

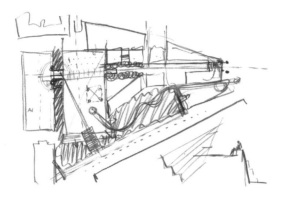

An early conceptual sketch attempting the integration of new with old buildings to also shape formal and informal public spaces.

Watercolour rendering of the final master plan for the City Hall complex, Jerusalem.

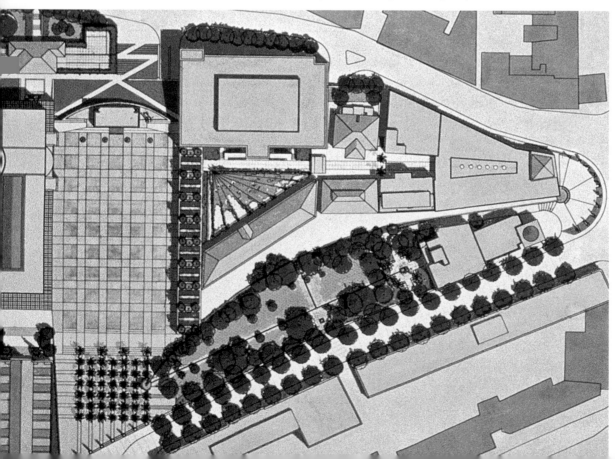

A nineteenth-century building is framed by the colonnade of the New City Hall.

The penultimate gateway on the path sequence leading from the Jaffa Gate to the main entrance doors to the City Hall. Note the deep shadow portico — a welcoming gesture in the hot Mideast sun — and the shadow patterns of pergola and perforated stone.

The building uses the contrasting scales of the side street and the rhythm of historic Halifax residential streets in contemporary form.

The graduate and undergraduate lounges face the courtyard.

MARION MCCAIN FACULTY OF ARTS AND SOCIAL SCIENCES BUILDING, DALHOUSIE UNIVERSITY, HALIFAX, NOVA SCOTIA

The Marion McCain Building, located within the heart of Dalhousie University, brings together six academic departments that constitute the Faculty of Arts and Social Sciences. The departments were previously accommodated in a series of converted houses on the outskirts of the university campus. While most of the old houses were in poor physical condition, they promoted interaction between faculty and students as well as providing each department with its own identity. In the new building, each department retains its identity in a group of "houses" that also reflect the historical pattern of Halifax streets. These linked compartments are arranged around a courtyard, thus combining the individual parts within a collective whole.

The front of the building contains two large lecture halls and several classrooms for general university use. This component of the building, in contrast to the "houses" on the side streets, is on University Avenue, the formal axis of the campus where larger-scale buildings have a more formal character, in keeping with their context, and are faced with stone masonry.

Each of the six departments of the faculty, accommodated in "houses," has an internal, independent staircase.

BANK STREET BUILDING COMPETITION, PARLIAMENT HILL, OTTAWA, ONTARIO

The design for the Bank Street Building is grounded in landform, vehicular circulation, visual axes and the landscape of the Parliamentary Precinct in Ottawa. The escarpment edge is extended to the west and north to form a new Terrace and belvedere overlooking the Ottawa River. The Terrace is a place for receptions, public art and commemorative statuary. A new Parliamentary Promenade connects the Upper and Lower Precinct. Internally, a Public Hall connects town and crown, providing a place of meeting and informal gathering outside Committee rooms and Senate offices. A three-storey reception hall, clad in translucent onyx quarried in Sault Ste. Marie, glows in the evening, a warm beacon in the cold Ottawa winter.

The Committee Rooms' floors are wide planks of first-growth white oak cut from sunken old-growth timber harvested from the Ottawa River at the base of the site. Walls of Committee Rooms and all public areas are clad using a hierarchy of old-growth timber species also harvested from the Ottawa River. The building is clad on the lower floors in locally quarried Nepean sandstone in random coursed rubblework. The rubblework and the corner quoins are executed to match the West Block of the Parliament Buildings. The upper floors are clad in revealed copper and deep glass sunshades to control heat from the sun.

The building was designed to be a national model of sustainable design. The environmental design allowed natural ventilation, individual temperature control and significant energy savings.

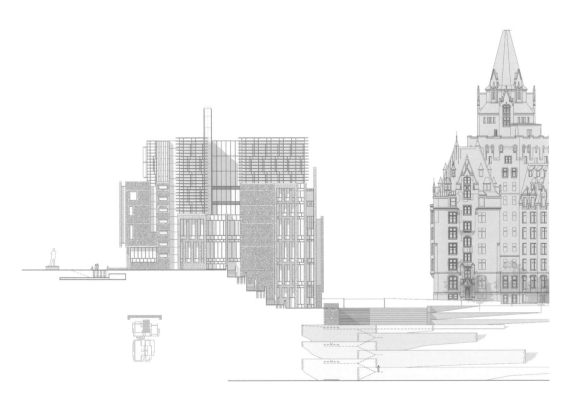

North elevation with Confederation Building on the right.

The new Parliamentary Promenade rises to the upper Terrace, the Mackenzie Tower and Parliament Hill.

THE JEWISH COMMUNITY CENTER
IN MANHATTAN, NEW YORK, NEW YORK

Situated in one of the country's most storied historic neighbourhoods, The Jewish Community Center contributes to the maintenance of a healthy urban fabric. Glazing is heavily emphasized on the lower floors of the structure, and the large windows not only offer a view of the activities inside but give the building a glow at street level that is visible from blocks away. Although the building is contemporary, it takes its cues in massing and articulation from the former tenement buildings that are common in the area.

Because of the constrictions of the centre's 30-metre by 30-metre site, the program was organized vertically. The gross floor area of 12,000 square metres elegantly accommodates a wide array of activities spread over thirteen above-grade floors. Each cluster of related uses – library, meditation and study spaces, and sport and fitness facilities – is grouped and interconnected throughout the building. The centre represents a template for the design of complex public buildings in dense urban areas – one that is contextual, unimposing in footprint and aesthetically pleasing.

The design of exterior facades narrate a variety of internal functions while still maintaining a cohesive whole.

The stairs to the below-grade theatre and craft workshops bring light to the lower levels.

The black exterior brick is anything but black in the ever-changing light.

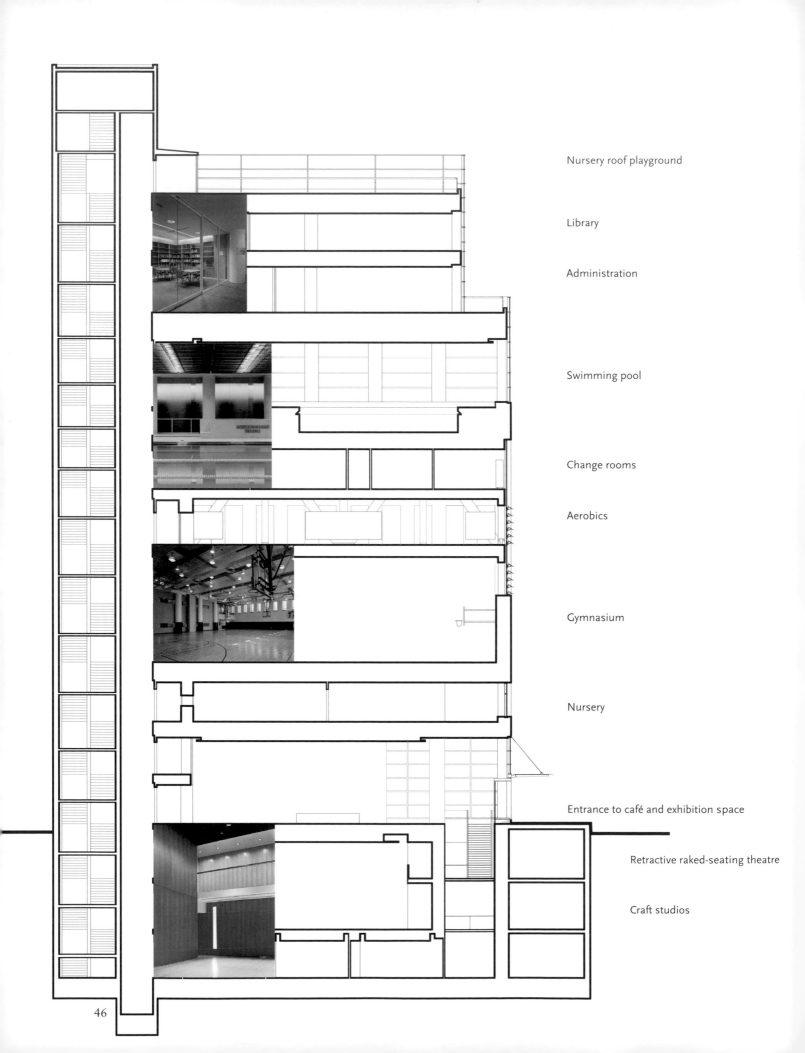

Nursery roof playground

Library

Administration

Swimming pool

Change rooms

Aerobics

Gymnasium

Nursery

Entrance to café and exhibition space

Retractive raked-seating theatre

Craft studios

46

Floor-to-ceiling glass on the seventh storey offers views of the Manhattan skyline for swimmers.

GERSTEIN SCIENCE INFORMATION CENTRE
MASTER PLAN AND RENOVATIONS, UNIVERSITY OF TORONTO, ONTARIO
The Gerstein Science Library comprised three wings constructed in 1893 and 1912.
With the Sigmund Samuel addition in 1952, it was essentially a warehouse for books
and had become a disorienting, dysfunctional and inadequate facility. Fronting onto the
university's main campus common, the Library turned its back on the city, one of the
principal gateways to the campus and the historic topography of its surroundings.

The master plan for the library set out a phased strategy of interior renovation, restoration of heritage reading rooms and construction of a new wing. The Morrison Pavilion, only 9 metres wide, extends the full length and height of all five floors and forms a new facade on the forgotten ravine east of the building. Limestone cladding and new bay windows emulate the material and proportion of the 1912 wing.

New reading rooms at each floor bring 650 new student seats into daylight and provide views to the landscape and the city. Book stacks are consolidated in the relatively windowless interior. A new continuous stair between the existing facade and the new wing provides a clear, visible connection between all five floors. This design adds only 11 per cent to the area of the library but creates a 70 per cent increase in student study places, a 50 per cent increase in collection space and a 20 per cent expansion in staff accommodation.

A new stair rises through a vertiginous space between the existing building on the left and the new pavilion layer on the right.

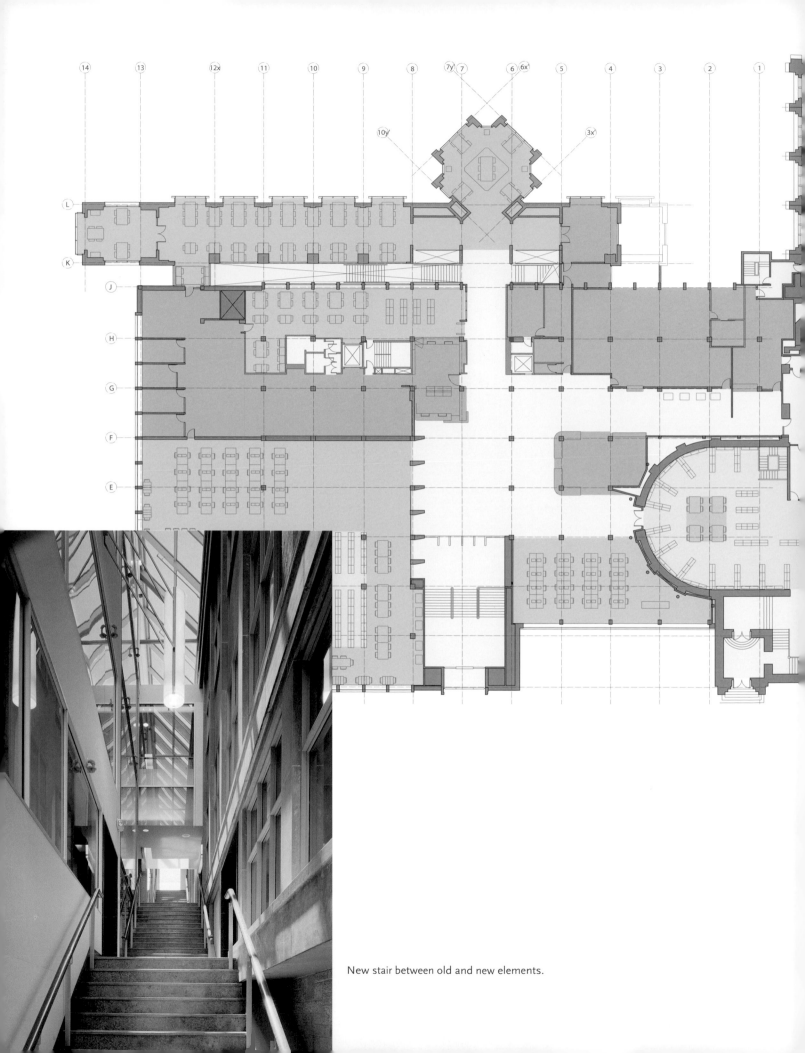

New stair between old and new elements.

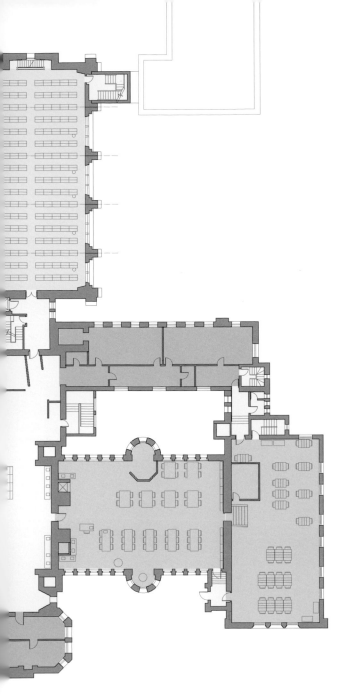

Student reading room.

Proposed restoration of heritage reading room.

THE BANFF CENTRE CAMPUS MASTER PLAN AND IMPLEMENTATION, BANFF, ALBERTA

The Banff Centre is situated within Banff National Park, a UNESCO World Heritage Site. It is an interdisciplinary campus and a global leader for creative excellence and innovation in aesthetic, social, economic, political, environmental and scientific fields.

In 2004, Diamond and Schmitt Architects were commissioned to develop a master plan for the campus that would provide an integrated system of roadways, walkways, signage and infrastructure. The plan preserves the natural landscape and wildlife habitat while providing a functional campus and accommodating the projected growth of both the program and the recreational facilities.

Phase one of the master plan, the Sally Borden Centre, was completed in July, 2007. Set in the rugged mountain landscape, the delicate, glazed addition to the existing Sally Borden Centre is a beacon of light in the campus. Placed at the midpoint of a steeply inclined site, the dining facilities provide an accessible centre for informal meeting for the attendees of a wide variety of arts programs.

Master plan diagram.

360° vistas are provided by the continuous glazing.

The new dining rooms afford spectacular views of the majestic Rockies, which rise from the grandeur of the Bow Valley.

Man-made crisp forms are in contrast to the rock and pine of the natural landscape.

The Individual to the Collective: Shaping the City

With the advent of globalization, the importance of the nation-state has retreated while the significance of the city has grown.

With the advent of globalization, the importance of the nation-state has retreated. Today, cities are the world's economic engines, the centres of culture, education and innovation. Yet most cities aren't really a third level of government but wards of the provinces or states – a glorified utility with limited autonomy and political authority to deal effectively with problems of decaying infrastructure, inadequate public transportation and sprawl. Consequently, urban planning decisions are often hindered by inefficient bureaucracy spread over several levels of government (federal, provincial, regional and municipal). To build good cities, there is a need not just for political will but for a clearly articulated power structure. It is also necessary to understand how cities are formed, how they work and why they often fail.

Cities are organized in several ways. Some have structure imposed in a grand manner, such as Baron Haussmann's Paris and Pierre L'Enfant's Washington, D.C., which have coordinated vistas and comprehensively planned streets, varying from wide boulevards to narrow residential streets. Other cities, such as London, are developed in a circular composition in the Renaissance style, radiating from a focal point at the centre. The most common planning template for North American cities is the grid. The grid has been used through the centuries by Roman administrators, Chinese emperors, Aztec priests and colonial land surveyors to bring order to settlements. Most Canadian cities began as colonial trading outposts and expanded to accommodate growing populations, marching slowly in several directions over an imposed grid.

Toronto's supergrid follows the surveyor's boundaries that originally divided Toronto into four 100-acre farms and now reflects the main traffic arteries and subway lines. There is a hierarchy to its layout. The highest building densities are found at the intersections of the supergrid, which are marked by subway stations, shops and regional services. These structures are bastions against noise for the small-scale residential areas that lie behind the arterial roads. There the city's smallest streets are found, serving a variety of low-scale residential uses. Relief to the grid is provided by nature: A ravine system traverses the metropolis in contrast to the grid, as waterways dictated millennia ago. As a result, Toronto is comprised of a series of centres.

This makeup provides Toronto and other multicentred cities with a greater potential for growth than unicentred cities. Expansion in unicentred cities inevitably replaces the once stable residential areas that surrounded the city core. The aggregate circumference of the core of a multicentred city is greater than that of a unicentred city. In the multicentred city, each subcore tends towards specialized regional functions, so access is not focused in one location and

61

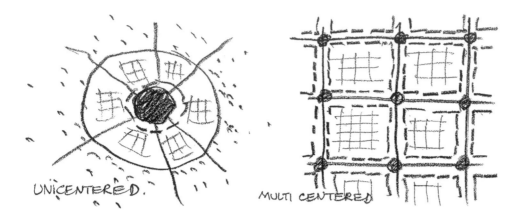

UNICENTERED.

MULTI CENTERED

The unicentred city – limited central expansion potential without severe disruption and arterial road sclerosis. The multicentred city – far greater potential for expansion of its dense sub-centres, with comparatively less disruption than with that of the unicentered model. Transportation loads are distributed between many alternate arterial roads, with public transit stops at sub-centre intersections. This allows for regional specialization and greater accessibility. Arterial roads, in turn, support local services at mid-densities that buffer low-density residential hinterlands.

arterial streets are less congested.

The benefits of Toronto's grid end near the shore of Lake Ontario. The construction in the 1960s of the Gardiner Expressway, an elevated highway that runs parallel to the lakeshore, became an almost insurmountable physical and psychological barrier between the city and its waterfront – a planning decision that has reverberated for decades. The issue of what to do with the waterfront has vexed the city for thirty years, and a series of governments, schemes, committees and acronyms have come and gone in the process. In this political vacuum, an ad hoc series of residential, commercial and institutional buildings have been built, which sit isolated from the city – and often from one another, too. For better and for worse, cities are shaped by their primary modes of transportation and communication.

Generally, main arteries don't support residential developments, but in a commuter society they have appeal, despite the obvious drawbacks of noise, pollution and dismal view. Many large condominium projects are situated along Toronto's major highways, where commuters have traded some of the traditional attributes of neighbourhoods for ready access to a major thoroughfare. In these niche neighbourhoods, the scale of the complexes increases to match the scale of the highway, accentuating the separation and alienation. This kind of development is neither urban nor suburban but a sort of fortress that stands between the two. It is a community based solely on the demand for a very specific need, and one that further reinforces dependency on the automobile.

Still, planned communities offer no guarantee of success. In 1953, Toronto's Regent Park, Canada's largest public-housing project, began construction amid a sense of tremendous optimism. "Down came the verminous walls, the unclean, unhealthy rooms," said the narrator of a documentary on the development. "And down came the fire hazards, the juvenile delinquency, the drunkenness, the broken marriages. And up rose something new, the nation's first large-scale public-housing project." Regent Park closed off the streets and created large open spaces, which, the planners argued, offered a sense of ventilation and freedom. But closing the area to traffic made it a perfect environment for criminals to operate in with impunity, and the communal green spaces soon evolved into a no man's land that was not owned by anyone and was controlled by the strongest. The logic of the plan was admirable, but instead of being ventilated by green space Regent Park became isolated and dangerous. Its perceived strengths turned out to be its downfall.

Rectifying the problem has led to a multibillion-dollar redevelopment of Regent Park. Once more it is being razed, with new multi-use buildings and a reinstatement of the simple urban grid. The connective tissue of the street and sidewalk is

Rockefeller Plaza: The public place as citizen's performance space and sophisticated urban theatre in a space defined by the surrounding buildings.

as important as public space, safer than parks and a key social ingredient of urban life. Instead of being solely a public-housing development, the new version will include a mixture of private and public housing and an economic range that goes from low to high income. It will also include retail and commercial buildings to increase pedestrian traffic flow, to bring life to the streets.

Public space is critical to a city's health, providing a place for the city to see itself. Architects didn't invent the agora; they merely formalized the dynamic of a natural meeting place. Certain physical elements must be in place and arranged in particular proportions for people to meet, congregate and interact. Economic and cultural forces affect how these places are used, and they can prosper or stagnate. Few things are more desolate than a failed public space. Public spaces that don't work, parks and plazas that stubbornly remain empty and forlorn, often result from the absence of certain fundamental connections. They are neither intersections nor destinations, and the occasional concert, art show or craft market provides only cosmetic relief for what is basically a structural problem: There is no real reason to be there.

Successful planning provides a necessary context for architecture. There is a need for enlightened government support and action, for innovative thinking and for a vision that embraces the long term rather than the immediate timetables of commercial interests. The city plan is a foundation – and even the best buildings will suffer without a strong base.

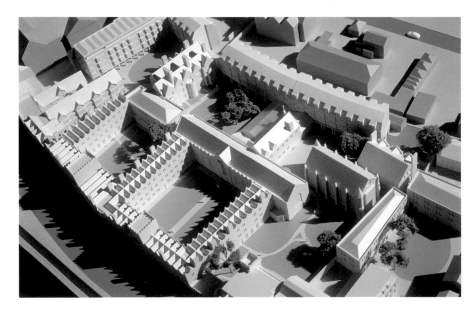

University College Master Plan, Oxford University: The master plan for University College, Oxford, introduces contemporary equivalents to historical forms in order to complete the Radcliffe Court and to create new quadrangles. The quadrangles are linked to give coherence to the overall ensemble.

Allston Campus Master Plan Proposal, Harvard University: The designers used the riverfront for development, lining the existing arterial streets south of the river with good sidewalks and introducing a mix of academic and community uses. With the addition of pedestrian bridges, the Harvard University campus could be extended and rendered cohesive, as well as integrating with the surrounding Allston neighbourhood.

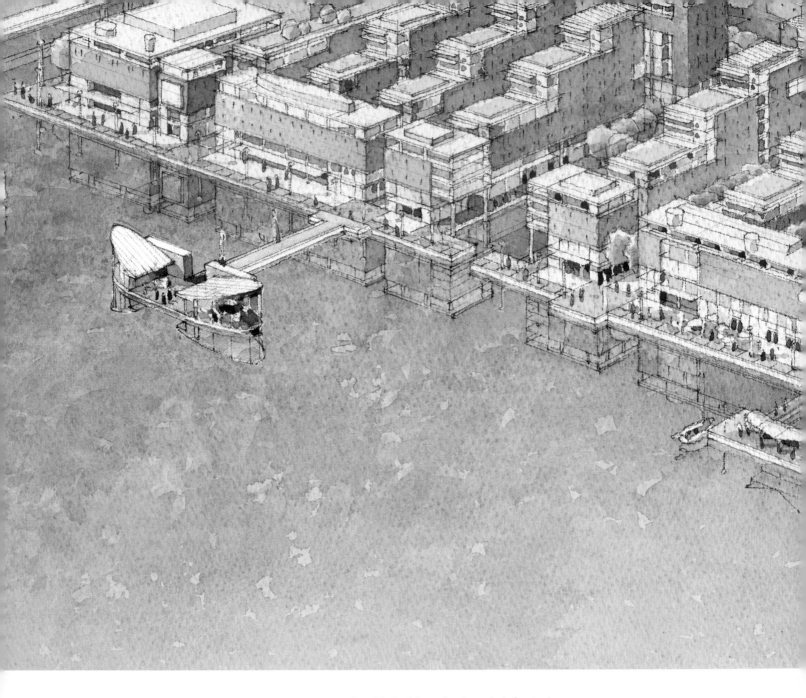

New water courts are enclosed by buildings that have their feet in the water.

EAST BAYFRONT MASTER PLAN PROPOSAL, TORONTO, ONTARIO

This proposal is designed to integrate the waterfront with the rest of the city, and it consists of low- and medium-rise buildings that are a mix of residential, retail and other uses. It is built on an extension of the Toronto street grid system and is tied directly into the existing public transit system. The buildings and the waterfront are closely allied in small-scale open spaces. This link is particularly relevant in winter, when it helps to modify the microclimate. The illustration to the left shows one example in which the buildings enclose a water court.

TEDCO'S CORUS BUILDING, TORONTO, ONTARIO

Corus Entertainment, a media corporation, are the tenant of the first of the buildings that will begin the implementation of Toronto's waterfront regeneration. Given its television and radio activity and its twenty-four-hour operation, it is ideally suited to be the catalyst of a lively urban waterfront. By exposing radio and television studios, the building will provide endless fascination to the public. By providing sliding doors to the principal TV studio, the studio can become a sound stage for audiences informally accommodated in the adjacent park. The atrium, which serves to break the bulk of the large (over 50,000 square metres) building down to a smaller scale, also accommodates a sound stage that on occasion can be used for public performances.

LOS ALAMOS CIVIC CENTER, LOS ALAMOS, NEW MEXICO

Los Alamos is located in the New Mexico desert, 2,225 metres above sea level on the Pajarito plateau just below the rim of the Jemez Caldera. The building site is in the heart of the central business district, adjacent to a large pond and grassy park. The exterior of the Los Alamos Civic Center is designed to reflect the character and landscape of the area; a base of rugged red sandstone defines the corner edges of the buildings, while steel and timber trellises provide shade. Zinc cladding creates a light and elegant enclosure to upper areas of the building, and it is combined with energy-efficient glass that is placed to maximize the dramatic mountain views. The centre includes a 700-seat theatre, outdoor amphitheatre, banquet and meeting hall, community restaurant, sixteen-lane bowling alley and public access television station. Most important, the design is woven together with courts, covered arcades and a verandah, which provide support for casual public gathering and a focus for community life.

Court, amphitheatre and verandah overlook a park and the distant desert mountains.

The surrounding landscape.

Sandstone, zinc, glass, and wood frame entrances in the bright desert light.

URBAN BLOCK REDEVELOPMENT,
REGENT PARK, TORONTO, ONTARIO

An extraordinary master plan for the revitalization of Regent Park prepared by Markson Borooah Hodgson Architects with Ken Greenberg and Associates combined both market and supported housing and the re-establishment of a permeable community and a street grid. The plan is being implemented by a partnership between the Toronto Community Housing Corporation and The Daniels Corporation.

In this first phase of market housing, the design is characterized by a mix of townhouses, urban apartments, and tower apartments designed to LEED (Leadership in Energy and Environmental Design) Gold Standard. A large food store, bank, and coffeehouse provide important community amenities, and the roof is landscaped as a green community park for residents. The food grown in rooftop nurseries and allotment gardens by residents may be sold in the food store. A four-storey winter garden is a gateway to the high-rise building and, with a green bio-filter wall, connects the food store, residents, the roof park and the public sidewalk.

All Together Now: The Compact City

The planning and building of cities has never been more crucial, because today's issues are not focused merely on aesthetics but on survival.

By 2015, there will be at least twenty-five cities with populations of 10 million or more. Africa is moving from a rural to an urban population at the fastest rate in history. Urbanization is the most powerful global demographic trend, and there is a pressing need to replenish architectural resources, to intensify the urban landscape, and to create compact cities rather than contribute to the growing sprawl. The planning and building of cities has never been more crucial. Today's issues are focused not just on aesthetics but on survival.

The arguments in favour of the compact city are social, environmental and economic: It is a more efficient use of land, and it inspires cultural diversity, social interaction and cohesion; the cores promote sustainable modes of transport, public transit, walking and cycling. The existing urban landscape in many cities is filled with the potential for development, some of it unrealized, some of it squandered. Toronto, for example, has an estimated 11,000 acres of vacant or underused land that could handle at least 250,000 new residents. Much of the regional infrastructure to support an increase in population (expressways, hospitals, sewer and water trunks) and the local infrastructure (local roads, schools, libraries) is already in place.

The trend against the compact city can be traced back to the Garden City movement and to William Levitt, who created Levittown sixty years ago. The largest planned community in America, it was sold as an affordable, idealized version of American life. Levitt's plan included schools, churches and stores, and the powerful allure of owning land. The suburbs were marketed with great optimism, offering an escape from the city and its attendant ills: crime, pollution and congestion.

They worked wonderfully for a brief historical moment. In Scarborough, an early suburb of Toronto, the 1950s and 1960s were prosperous times. Local people were employed in factories within the suburb, which produced refrigerators, thermoses, pharmaceuticals, washers, dryers and cosmetics, and the residents were then able to buy these products at the nearby Golden Mile Plaza. Here was the post-war model for success: near full employment, affordable housing and a viable working class that manufactured products locally and could afford to buy them. If this lifestyle was occasionally decried as boring, it was safe and thriving.

This symbiotic relationship began to break down in the 1970s, as the industry relocated to the less expensive edges of the city or shut down because of offshore competition. Now there are fewer jobs in the area. The population of Scarborough grew from 50,000 to 600,000, and what was once a homogeneous suburb became one of the most multicultural enclaves in the country (54 per cent are foreign born, compared to the national average of 19 per cent). Part of the allure of the suburban model was the idea of community, but without density many suburbs, including Scarborough, threaten to become places of social fragmentation, restlessness and ennui.

The suburbs were designed for a middle class that is quickly disappearing. In a detailed study titled "The Three Cities Within Toronto: Income Polarization Among Toronto Neighbourhoods, 1970–2000," University of Toronto researchers found that the core was becoming wealthier, the suburbs were getting poorer and the middle class was disappearing altogether. In 1970, two-thirds of the city was classified as middle income. Thirty years later, less than a third was defined as middle class, and the poor had more than doubled and now outnumbered them. Post-war suburbia is in rapid decline, and the core is becoming a wealthy and predominantly white bastion. The authors project that, if this trend continues, two-thirds of the city will be classified as poor by 2020 and will be located almost exclusively in the suburbs.

Some issues associated with poverty are exacerbated in the suburbs. Those in the suburbs without cars – whether as a result of age, infirmity or financial limitations – are effectively isolated. The age of the automobile, ironically, has created immobility. Those spaces that once seemed liberating are now problematic, and because of insufficient density, suburbs are often underserviced by public transit. A recent study by the Canadian Medical Association noted that obesity was a greater problem in the suburbs, where sidewalks are scarce, distances great and few people walk. The suburbs, initially sold as a healthy alternative to the city, have become unhealthy.

In the 1950s, William Levitt created Levittown in Pennsylvania, the largest planned community in America. His plan included low-density housing, schools, churches, and a shopping centre surrounded by parking lots.

Carcassonne, France: The whole city of Carcassonne could fit into the area occupied by a typical highway cloverleaf interchange.

Tract houses were often built quickly and cheaply, and neither their construction nor their materials are designed for longevity. If fuel prices continue to climb, the suburbs will become increasingly unviable, poised to become the ghettos of the future. This troubling scenario has long been the case in cities such as Paris, where the North African immigrant population lives in squalid northern suburbs, and in London, England, where West Indian and Muslim immigrants are grouped in suburban streets. There is less opportunity for acculturation on the fringes, and a greater chance for alienation. Increasingly, this, too, is a North American phenomenon.

One of the suburbs' initial attractions was – and remains – price. If you make cheap land available, people vote with their feet. Yet the cost of creating infrastructure, of bringing highways, roads and sewer trunk lines to the suburbs, is sometimes greater than the tax benefits that derive from them. In one southwest Ontario locale, for every dollar in assessment the municipality received for single-family homes on tract land, it paid $1.40 to service it. If you factor in less measurable costs, such as the pollution that results from commuting, the wear and tear on existing infrastructure, and the loss of productivity due to traffic congestion, the price of supporting suburban living becomes prohibitive. Moreover, the suburbs provide a pincer attack on sustainability. As transportation costs and environmental impact escalate, it is less and less viable, ecologically and economically, to ship produce from afar. But as suburbs consume forests and farmland, the possibility of growing local produce diminishes.

With suburban sprawl, life revolves around the shopping mall. Victor Gruen, whose Northland Shopping Center in Detroit, built in 1954, is credited as being the first mall, had noble intentions – to provide beauty, order and community to the formless suburbs. There are now more than 50,000 malls in North America, and they are escalating rapidly in number and scale.

Some outlet malls feature big-box stores situated around contiguous parking lots. Others are inner-city malls that have killed the surrounding retail landscape and then co-opted it: The streetscape becomes a continuation of the mall, replicating its chain stores quite some distance away. The mall continues to evolve, occasionally in interesting ways but more often in a generic march towards a city's fringe, reinforcing dependency on the automobile.

One of the obstacles to increased urbanization is the fact that early attempts at concentration were so unpalatable. In the 1960s, a number of high-rise developments replaced low-rise residential areas that had decayed beyond the point of reclamation. Zoning regulations of the period stipulated that the new buildings should be set well back from the sidewalk and should provide substantial off-street parking. As a result, they often broke down the ingredients that make livable streets – sidewalk, street tree, front lawn, open verandah, front door, house, back terrace, garden, carpark, lane – and created an irreparable gash in the community.

In Toronto, this trend resulted in areas like St. James Town, a collection of nineteen high-rise apartment buildings that house more than 17,000 residents – one of the country's most densely populated communities. Although the towers were originally designed in the early sixties to suit middle-class families, their isolation from life on the street and their distance from a range of desired amenities soon meant the development held little appeal to affluent residents. The area is now home to some of the city's poorest residents.

But intensifying isn't necessarily synonymous with height. It is possible to achieve a significant density in a low-rise form that conforms to the scale and continuity of the street and at the same time preserves the integrity of the neighbourhood. This was the case with our Beverley Place in Toronto. In the early 1970s, Ontario Hydro wanted to build a twelve-storey transformer station in the midst of an established downtown residential area and began to buy up properties. After the local community organized vociferously against the plan, Hydro withdrew and the City of Toronto's housing agency acquired the site. Zoning regulations still dictated deep setbacks and substantial parking requirements, thereby favouring new residential tower developments, but a different and happier solution was found when the planners and area residents worked together.

St. James Town, Toronto: Unrelenting high-rises with little attention to street life.

Beverley Place, Toronto: Streetscape, scale and urban texture continuity.

Beverley Place is a blend of low-rise buildings with high-density housing. The complex included the adaptive reuse of twelve existing Victorian houses along Beverley Street as multi-unit residences, along with a new single block-long building featuring street-facing row housing whose scale, material treatment and proportion integrate into the existing fabric. The project also demonstrated how city making is essentially a political process: We, as architects, not only challenged zoning and development bylaws but, by engaging in the vigorous community activism of the day, demonstrated the potential of architecture as a democratizing force.

Of course there is a place for high-rise building. Much of their success or failure in urban contexts is determined by the way in which they address the street and scale of relationship to their neighbours. Those that contribute to the continuity of the streetscape, introduce a mix of uses, such as retail, to animate the street and provide an informal surveillance, making this form of intensification entirely acceptable. An avoidance of too sharp a contrast with adjacent buildings further enhances their contribution to the urban form of cities in which they reside.

Governments too often advocate perversely destructive economic models for cities. Like medieval doctors treating anemic patients, they leach out their blood. So cities were diluted rather than supported. In the twenty-first century we share a social and environmental imperative to address these issues and an architectural responsibility to engage in the creation of compact cities, to view the city not just as a built artifact but as a living, evolving social organism.

SIDNEY HARMAN HALL, WASHINGTON, DISTRICT OF COLUMBIA

Sidney Harman Hall, the new home of the Shakespeare Theater Company, is a centrepiece in the revitalization of Washington, D.C.'s historic business district. The 775-seat performance space occupies the first five and a half floors of an eleven-storey office tower. The three-level glass facade, distinguished by a projected bay window, not only establishes the theatre's identity and purpose but directly links the activity within the public lobby areas to the vibrant outside environment.

The public spaces have been made as transparent as possible. Audiences gathering for a performance or in the lobbies at intermission are visible from the street, creating interest on the outside even as those inside have a fresh perspective of the surrounding city. The projecting glass lobby is designed for this purpose, affording oblique views of F Street. The simplicity of the structural glass bay windows, in contrast to the extensively articulated facades of the host office building and its neighbours, give distinction and identity to the theatre.

The transparency of the lobbies of the theatre affords patrons a new perspective of L'Enfant's Washington city plan and provides passersby a glimpse of the events within.

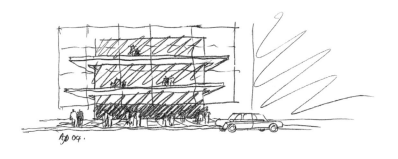

The theatre proper is a simple box form enclosed by an opaque wall. This chamber is acoustically and physically isolated from the transparent public spaces. The theatre is designed for maximum flexibility in both its acoustics and its physical configuration, as the stage can be changed from proscenium to thrust to theatre-in-the-round. To provide acoustic flexibility, variable acoustic curtains operate behind the slatted wood screens that line the auditorium. Predetermined acoustic configurations are designed for speech, classical and jazz music.

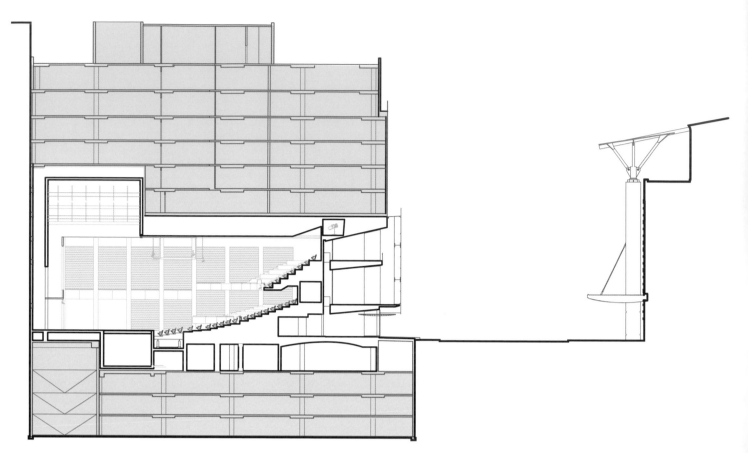

Section showing the integration of the theatre into the building, with parking below and office space above.

Stair connecting upper and lower lobbies.

Li Ka Shing Knowledge Institute at the corner of Victoria and Shuter Streets.

LI KA SHING KNOWLEDGE INSTITUTE, ST. MICHAEL'S HOSPITAL, TORONTO, ONTARIO

The Li Ka Shing Foundation has sponsored five centres across the globe, devoted to shortening the time between life-science discoveries and their clinical application. The St. Michael's Hospital Li Ka Shing Knowledge Institute comprises the Keenan Research Centre and the Li Ka Shing International Centre for Health Care Education. Designed as a physical embodiment of the sponsor's wishes, a series of meeting spaces join the two halves of the complex, encouraging interdisciplinary activity.

Replacing low-rise industrial buildings on a tight urban site with an intensely used high-rise development, the Li Ka Shing Knowledge Institute contributes to the compact city and reinforces the notion of the city as a crucial element of a vital knowledge-based economy.

Lobby of the Keenan Research Centre.

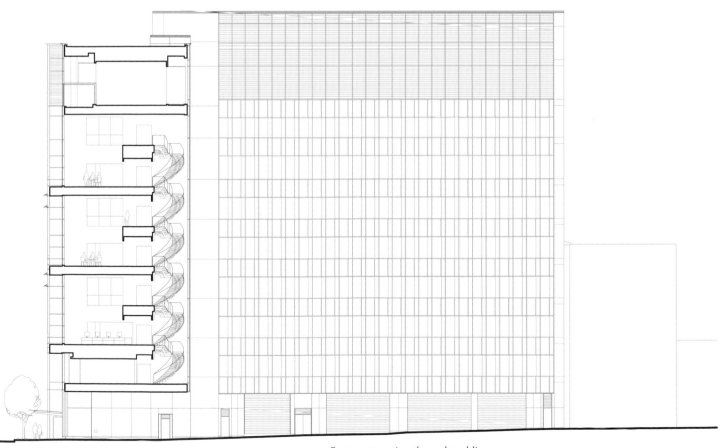

East-west section through public spaces.

THE HUDSON CONDOMINIUMS,
TORONTO, ONTARIO

The Hudson is situated in a dense urban neighbourhood on a corner site. To the south, King Street, 20 metres wide, is bounded by four- and six-storey brick warehouses. To the west, Spadina Avenue, 36 metres wide, is lined with twelve- and fifteen-storey buildings.

The design combines a twenty-one-storey glass-clad tower with fifteen-storey masonry-clad wings. Continuous retail space at the street level opens to the sidewalk and a street café.

Robust masonry with deep shade and shadow recalls the muscular brick buildings of this urban industrial neighbourhood.

WAYS LANE, TORONTO, ONTARIO

This single-family residence on Ways Lane demonstrates a high standard of residential accommodation on underused and abandoned sites along Toronto's midblock laneways, just as it also provides utility, repose and delight for the occupants.

The site measures 8 by 11 metres and accommodates a house of 135 square metres. Generous living spaces, good natural light and proportion combine with three bedrooms, an onsite parking space, a garden court and a roof deck to create an exceptional and compact house.

The L-shaped house plan interlocks with the L of the garden court, and the residential wings form a protective wall to the public lane to provide privacy, security and controlled access. The interior courtyard has planting and sitting areas and a water garden. The quiet and repose of the courtyard flows seamlessly to the interior. Each room has windows that open onto the court and a pivot door that provides access. The windows are placed to capture local and distant views and to follow the movement of the sun.

CHARLIE CONDOMINIUMS, TORONTO, ONTARIO

Sited in one of Toronto's brick industrial districts, this design combines a six-storey low-rise building clad in black brick masonry and glass with a slender thirty-two-storey tower. The seventh-floor roof deck provides an outdoor swimming pool, urban terrace and a club for residents.

MINTO LONSDALE CONDOMINIUMS, TORONTO, ONTARIO

Terminating a boulevard of modernist mid-rise apartments, this condominium building overlooks the parklike grounds of an adjacent private school. The pinwheel plan for the structure rotates against the corner geometry of the site to gain views and reduce the apparent mass. Each wing has a different height to enhance its slim silhouette and create a roofscape of interest. Designed to the LEED (Leadership in Energy and Environmental Design) Gold standard, the glass-clad tower is perched above two-storey stone-clad townhouses.

A model of the complex, woven between historic and modern structures, above an existing parking garage and below the view plane of the city as seen from Mount Royal.

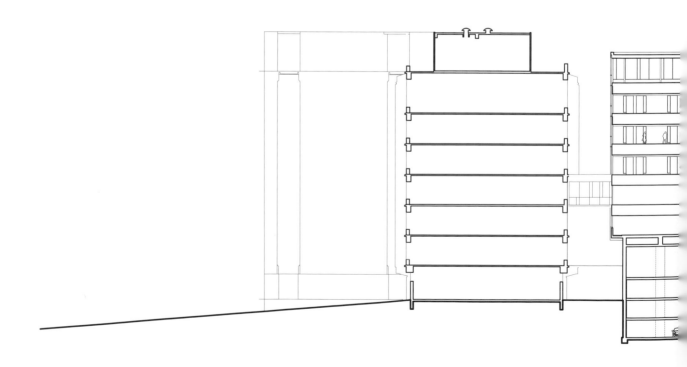

LIFE SCIENCES COMPLEX, MCGILL UNIVERSITY, MONTREAL, QUEBEC

The Life Sciences Complex at McGill University acts as a hub that links the Faculty of Medicine's McIntyre Building and the Science Faculty's Stewart Building. The building houses elements of both departments, enhancing interaction between the disciplines. The facility comprises the Cancer Research Institute and the Francesco Bellini Building, and it is situated on the slopes of Mount Royal.

The complex is organized into three distinct components. The first consists of wet- and dry-bench laboratories and local support spaces such as staff offices, group meeting rooms and equipment rooms, which are designed to allow a degree of customization based on the users' needs. The second is a series of stacked core-equipment spaces, which are extremely flexible in their internal division, with higher structural loading capacity. They are serviced electrically and mechanically to allow rapid reconfiguration with minimum disruption, as emerging technologies are implemented.

The third component is an animal resource centre with a capacity of 22,000 cages in ventilated racks connected to the building's exhaust system. The animal resource centre has an integrated bio-safety level three facility, a quarantine suite and a transgenic suite. They occupy the lower levels of the building, which have been carved into the granite mountainside. Although partially below grade, corridors and laboratories within the animal facility still have access to natural daylight.

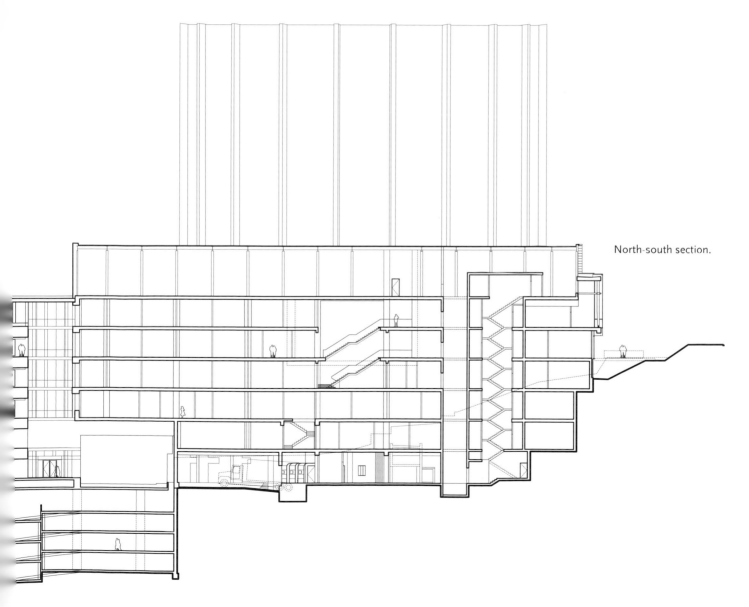

North-south section.

An Inner Order: Beauty Is More Than Skin Deep

Aesthetics without plan order can be the architectural equivalent of a circus tent, a seductive structure that has only one purpose — to draw crowds into it.

Mies van der Rohe's German pavilion at the 1929 Barcelona International Exhibition became a classic modernist structure, even though it was intended to be a temporary building and was torn down less than a year after its construction (it was rebuilt to the original design in 1986). The building's main function was to accommodate a reception for the King and Queen of Spain. Its only exhibits were the chairs and tables Mies had designed – furniture that has become classic. Ironically, Mies commented at the time, "To tell you the truth, nobody ever used them." The building itself was an exhibit, and its elegant aesthetic was widely praised. The walls were freestanding marble screens that promoted an easy flow of people through the building; there were no rooms in the conventional sense of enclosed spaces with a single entrance. The Barcelona Pavilion was a poetic expression of the deconstruction of the room as a defined space, a radical plan that defied architectural convention. But that is not the same as a lack of plan.

The calibration of space can be as carefully organized as a musical composition – a comprehensive theme that is expressed by variations in rhythm and sequence. Depending on the desired effect, there are minor variations or dramatic contrasts in scale, character and levels of illumination. Architecture without plan order can be the equivalent of a circus tent, a distinctive and seductive structure that has only one purpose – to draw crowds into it.

The interior has to deliver on the promise of the shell. If a museum's spaces are too idiosyncratic, the burden of making them work is passed on to the exhibit designers. If there isn't a comprehensible plan order, the task of way-finding falls to the visitor.

The Salk Institute, La Jolla, California: Louis Kahn's place-making creates distinctions among the "served space" of laboratories used for research, the "servant spaces" used for building mechanicals and the public spaces used for gathering. The two laboratory buildings, accentuated by a linear waterway running between them, frame a view of the Pacific Ocean, giving order to chaos, significance to context, and poetry to form.

mercy of the corporate plan. The buildings themselves are generic warehouses; they are defined by their plan order.

There is a relationship, for better or for worse, between a building and its users. For the relationship to last, there needs to be depth and subtlety and purpose. Mere beauty soon grows familiar to the lover and fades in the eye, as the eighteenth-century essayist and poet Joseph Addison warned three hundred years ago.

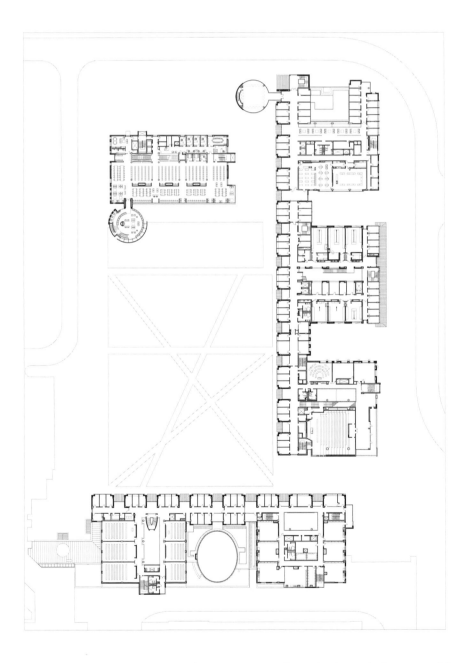

Library and buildings, University of Ontario Institute for Technology: The language of the plan articulates structure and partition, services and rooms. The buildings shape outdoor rooms and form narrates the internal function.

Faculty, students and staff are connected around an interior court at the Computer Science and Engineering Building, University of Michigan.

THE ESPLANADE: ARTS AND HERITAGE CENTRE, MEDICINE HAT, ALBERTA

Situated in downtown Medicine Hat on the edge of the city's institutional precinct, the Arts and Heritage Centre is the city's premier cultural facility. Addressing three objectives, the Esplanade has a significant public presence that is also integrated into the community, contains exceptional display and performance spaces, and brings layers of meaning to the experience of the city's heritage and arts.

Conceived as an orderly arrangement of large rooms, the centre emphasizes the importance of public space and natural light. The two major components are the 700-seat performing arts theatre and a 650-square-metre museum and art gallery with archival facilities. A clerestory lantern over the Great Hall brings light to the interior and acts as a beacon of light in the cityscape. Within the lantern is a helical stair that gives access to the roof terrace, providing panoramic views of the South Saskatchewan River and the prairie beyond.

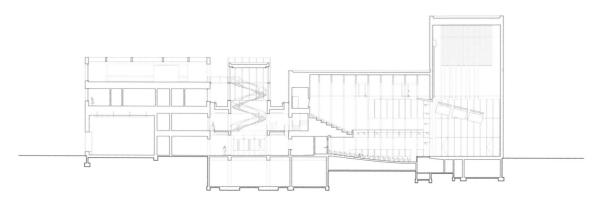

East-west section: Art Gallery, Public Forum, Rooftop Belvedere and Theatre.

Esplanade Theatre: The alignment between the on-stage reflectors and the side balconies in the 700-seat auditorium creates a "one-room" environment, visually and acoustically tuned for orchestral performance. Both ceiling and side reflectors can be stored away to re-establish the proscenium for dramatic productions. Individual planks in the beech paneling are arranged in a quadratic residue pattern and finished with textured lacquer to provide diffusion and warmth of tone.

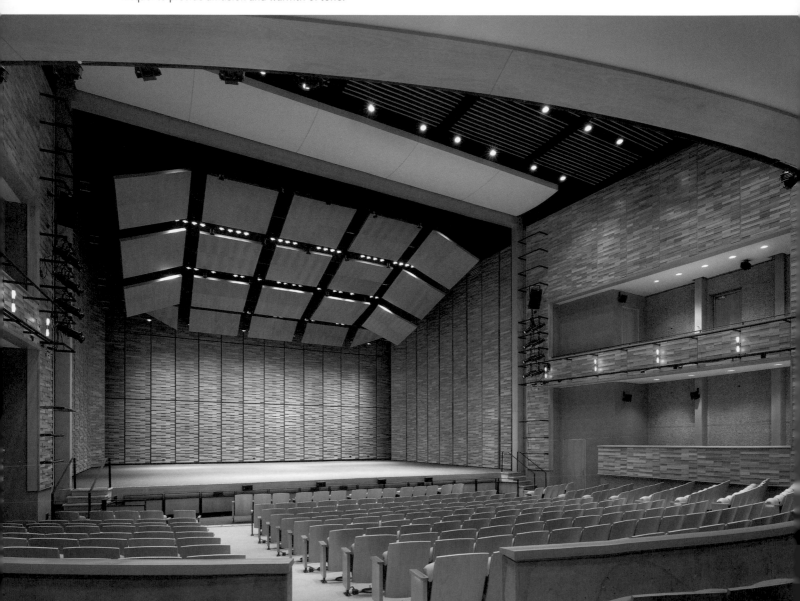

The Art Gallery with a view to the lobby spaces.

RICHMOND HILL CENTRAL LIBRARY,
RICHMOND HILL, ONTARIO

Housing 170,000 volumes and occupying over 1,951 square metres, the library serves as a key component of the Richmond Hill Civic Centre. The building accommodates an advanced level of technology to allow for computerized cataloguing and retrieval and for online access to all library branches in the system as well as the centralized provincial catalogue. Fundamental to the design is a high level of integration between structural, mechanical and electrical systems.

Double structural beams house the air-conditioning ducts and the power and communications systems. All are easily accessed via hinged soffits between the beams. The quadruple columns calibrate the spaces of the library and also indicate the locations of the electronic catalogues.

While natural light is harmful to printed materials, it is an essential ingredient in achieving satisfying and humane buildings. The library is designed with numerous windows and open spaces and the light is filtered or screened wherever necessary. Provision has been made for both vertical and horizontal growth: The structure allows for another floor of construction, and the plan for future outwards expansion.

The south facade, with elements that give scale at a distance and at close approach.

The reading room.

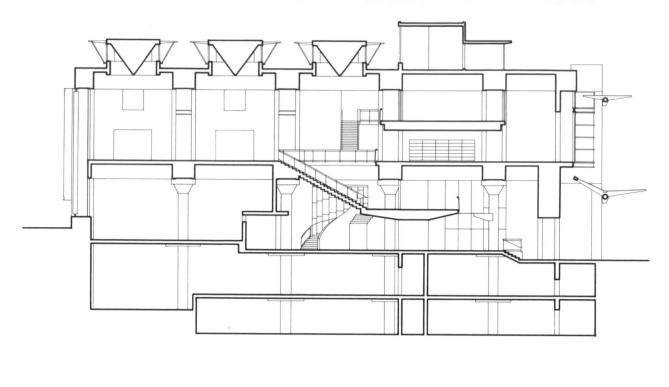

North-south section.

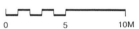

0   5   10M

Third-floor plan.

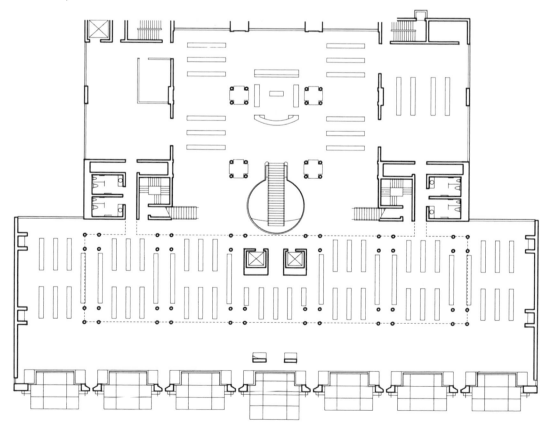

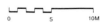

0   5   10M

The structure houses mechanical services and is used to calibrate space, modulate light and mark places of study and information reference.

Interior court.

INTEGRATED SCIENCES BUILDING, DREXEL UNIVERSITY, PHILADELPHIA, PENNSYLVANIA

An unusual, hybrid program combines bio-sciences research laboratories with teaching laboratories, lecture theatres (30, 60, 90 and 260 seats), and the renowned Steinbright Career Development Center. On five floors, all program functions are connected by an indoor court, which serves as both a crossroads and a gathering place for students, faculty and staff within the building, as well as the broader university community. The architecture of the court is delineated by its corner gateway to Drexel and to the diagonal Woodland Walk, which connects Drexel University and the University of Pennsylvania.

Site plan.

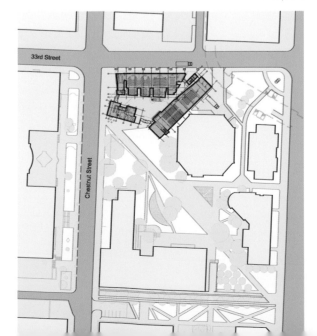

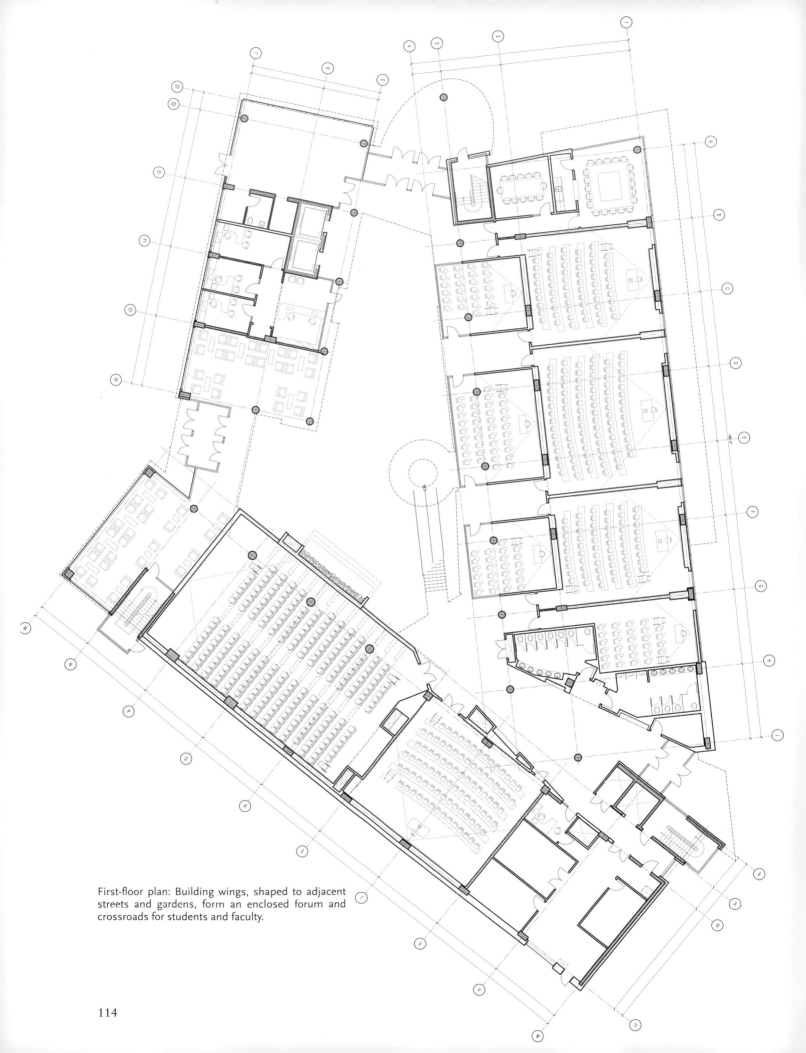

First-floor plan: Building wings, shaped to adjacent streets and gardens, form an enclosed forum and crossroads for students and faculty.

114

At 33rd Street and Chestnut Street, the new building is a gateway to Drexel University.

View from Woodland Walk and landscaped quadrangle.

Context plan: The new wing frames a rich heritage context and defines a new Civic Square, Market Square and Arts Court.

Interior civic court.

CAMBRIDGE CITY HALL, CAMBRIDGE, ONTARIO

The Cambridge City Hall is designed to redefine the civic precinct and to connect to the heritage town hall, originally constructed in 1857. The exemplary heritage buildings in the surrounding context include a fire hall, market, arts centre, federal building and town hall. The new wing reshapes urban space for market and civic squares, and makes new pedestrian connections between the city centre and neighbourhoods. A living bio-filter wall ensures indoor air quality and is part of a green design strategy to achieve LEED (Leadership in Energy and Environmental Design) Gold certification.

STUDENT CENTRE
YORK UNIVERSITY, TORONTO, ONTARIO

The Student Centre houses entertainment and food services, as well as spaces for student offices and clubs. It was created as a key link in a colonnade system that forms a continuous perimeter around the campus green.

The central feature of the building is the Great Hall, which includes dining and lounge areas. Three large elliptical openings in the upper two floors bring daylight into the hall and provide visual connections between the different levels of the centre. A helical staircase rises through one of the openings to the upper levels.

Beneath the Great Hall is a large campus pub that can accommodate more than 700 people. The multiple points of entry into the building from the colonnade link the main floor of the centre to outside campus activity.

Study model.

Dining hall.

118

Parts and Parcels: The Elements of Architecture

For Pythagoras, numbers were the language between god and man — architectural perfection was possible.

There is an old joke: "How do you make a bagel? First, you start with the hole." In architecture you *do* start with the hole – the space. Space is the central challenge: how to shape it, how to create a structure that communicates a building's purpose and satisfies its occupants' needs. A building begins to become architecture when its elements take shape and serve more than utilitarian purposes, when they resound culturally, aesthetically, geographically and logically with appropriate technology and with a second or third layer of meaning. Doors, windows, beams, floors, ceilings and staircases can profoundly affect our experience of a building.

People can often tell something about a country's justice system, for instance, by looking at the doors on its courthouses. Are they steel or wood? Recessed or proud? Sumptuous, delicate, intimidating or mundane? A door that is recessed provides protection from the rain and shade from the sun – a welcoming niche. A steel door that is flush with the wall announces security. A glass entry door conveys a message of welcome, access and display. Doorways are often the architectural focus of a building's exterior, and its themes and purpose can be communicated by the entryway.

What seems frivolous may have a function. Consider the gargoyle – that much-maligned architectural flourish. It crouches at the edges of medieval cathedrals, its stone face hovering above us. Gargoyles depict fantastic creatures and are often caricatures of the devil. Perhaps their symbolism was comforting: cleansing demons with rain from the heavens, or maybe reminding passers-by that the devil is never far away. They have become a metaphor for frivolity, but gargoyles are actually a functional element, designed to take water collected in the eaves and project it, through those angry mouths, away from the building.

Notre Dame, Paris: Water spouts, metamorphosed into gargoyles, an element of the integral decoration of medieval cathedrals.

The Don Jail, Toronto, Ontario: A facade of intimidation: no welcoming portico, coarse rustication, and little shadow relief.

The elaborate stained-glass windows in those cathedrals are also rooted in function. While stained glass was a powerful means to create the illumination of religious rapture, diffusing the light over religious images for an often illiterate congregation, it was also an elegant solution to the problem of controlling natural light in a place of worship, where an inner world prevailed. Stained-glass windows also served a role in reducing the heavy load of the cathedrals' stone walls on the buttresses, the glass being much lighter than stone. The much-admired grace and delicacy of the arched flying buttress derived from an economy of means, but it was based on structural necessity.

Windows have a variety of functions: they are used as framing devices, as ventilation, as light providers and as filters of light. How they are used is often indicated by their size and shape. The windows in an adobe house in the desert are small, to keep out the heat and glare. They act like the iris of an eye in bright light, squinting in compensation. The windows on medieval castles were narrow slits on the exterior, presenting an impenetrable wall. On the inside, however, the slits opened to a comfortable width, giving the soldiers room to operate weapons and making the most of reflected light from the splayed walls.

The way a view is framed is critical to how its inhabitants see the outside world. Windows determine the relationship between inside and outside. In Frank Lloyd Wright's Kentuck Knob House in Pennsylvania, one window is frameless: the glass is fitted into the rock, giving the impression there is no glass. The intent was to erase the visual barrier between outdoors and indoors, to engage with the natural site. The picture window in many suburban homes frames the interior as much as it provides an exterior view. People see it as a showcase, a place to display their lives.

The first glazed windows were used by the Romans 2,000 years ago, although they weren't in wide use until the thirteenth century, and then mostly in churches. It wasn't until the sixteenth century that they were adapted to houses in significant numbers. Early panes were small and held together by leadwork. Now it is possible to produce glazed windows of almost any size, shape and thickness. There is glass that filters out harmful light. The result is soaring, beautiful spaces – atria and facades that would have been impossible a few decades ago. But as with any technological advance, there can also be an unhealthy reliance on it to solve all of our problems.

On a commercial level, for instance, windows have lost their traditional property of ventilation, as they are often sealed in hotels and office buildings. This inflexibility leaves the occupants vulnerable during mechanical failures, and, in general, it increases energy bills and contributes to the problems of unhealthy interior air. Once again, the technology has given us something, but it has also taken something away. Individuals have lost control over their immediate environment.

Staircases are one of the most expressive elements in architecture, ranging from the purely functional to grand statements like Gianlorenzo Bernini's Scala Regia, leading from St. Peter's Basilica to the papal apartments in the Vatican Palace. Bernini inherited a narrow, awkwardly shaped site for the staircase, which

The Foreign Ministry, Jerusalem, Israel: Tall columns that impart status, light used to literally lighten and teak screens both define the room and act as a second tier of shrapnel protection, in case of explosion.

had to carry a heavy symbolic weight. He designed a wide set of stairs with a shallow rise and to accentuate their drama he flanked them with a series of columns that were taller at one end. They provide an ingenious perspective that makes the staircase look both longer and less steep than it really is.

Stairs against a wall can separate streams of people from the crowd. Or – situated in the centre of a space – they can be a meeting place, bringing people together. Traversing the levels of a building, they are a conduit for information. Staircases are a natural meeting place, whether they are the steps to the Public Library in New York or the stairs of the Piazza di Spagna in Rome. Peter the Great used the staircase of the opera house in St. Petersburg for receptions at his annual levee. Staircases are perfectly formed for sitting and they offer an elevated view. In cities around the world, people eat lunch, take in the sun and wait for friends on public steps. What had been intended as a formal processional experience for earlier generations has been democratized, converted to an informal meeting area.

In large developer-built houses, a grand staircase is often used to bestow status on the house. A large winding stair that looms above when you open the front door has a dramatic effect. It is a marketing tool, relatively inexpensive and surprisingly effective. The opulent staircase suggests that the lives in that house will be elevated, as well. At a very different residential site, the large stone staircases to brownstones in New York attract people to sit on them – an outward expression of the neighbourhood and one of its primary modes of social interaction. Most important, stairs and ramps are physical connectors of the different levels of a building, garden or even a city. Movement from level to level, a kinetic experience, dramatically changes the perspective of the spaces through which stairs are suspended. Turns in a staircase can convey surprise, give useful pauses in ascent and descent and, if generous enough, become places to sit – social unifiers.

Floors range from simple unvarnished pine to the mosaic floor of the fourteenth-century Duomo di Siena, one of the most elaborate floors in Italy. The floor took two centuries to complete and represents the work of dozens of artists and craftsmen. The designs and scenes that are depicted in its mosaics express the ecclesiastic themes of the cathedral and provide a historical narrative of the city. Other narratives are less ornate. A Japanese spa in San Francisco has polished concrete floors that complement the spare Zen interior, but they also recall the original purpose of the building – a mechanic's garage.

Columns are used as support devices or as decorative elements, where they convey a formality. But they can also calibrate a space and give it order, as Regency architect John Nash so ably achieved in London in the early nineteenth century. For the Greek philosopher Pythagoras, numbers were the language between god and man, and by using the right ratios and proportions, architectural perfection was possible. Doric columns had a height that was proportionate to the diameter of the column at its base. The slight bulge in the centre had no structural function but instead corrected an optical illusion: columns with straight sides appeared slightly concave when viewed from a distance. The diameter of a column can convey delicacy or gravity; it can heighten or shorten a room or deflect light. But there are other, less obvious uses too. Hollow columns can hold runoff water and distribute it to ponds or gardens or supply cool and warm air.

When materials are used in unconventional ways, they can often delight. Sheets of onyx, for example, emit light. In the day, light comes through the stone and provides a unique and dramatic light to the interior. In the evening, the light is emitted outward and the structure becomes a lantern. Each one has an unexpected effect and it is this kind of surprise, whether found in a handrail, door, ceiling, wall or beam, that can change the way a building is perceived and experienced.

If the parts become ends in themselves, if the delight in detail is not an extension of the language of the building itself, the result can be confusing. But when the whole is greater than the sum of the parts there can be a deep sense of architectural cohesion, of each variation contributing to the principal architectural theme – as in a great work of music.

The north pavilion at the University of Toronto's Bahen Centre is both a coda for the delicate glazing and robust masonry of the centre's architecture and a reflection of the retained Victorian house.

ALUMBRERA HOUSE, MUSTIQUE, THE GRENADINES

Alumbrera is located on Mustique, a privately owned island in the Grenadines, West Indies. The residence is a five-bedroom complex covering 112 square metres. It is organized as a series of smaller pavilions and recreational facilities, linked by landscaped gardens and terraces sited to take advantage of the views and the prevailing winds on the large hilltop site. Separate components include the living pavilion (with large areas for dining and entertaining), the bedroom pavilion, the guest-suite pavilion and the kitchen pavilion – all arranged around a central terrace. Site components include a carport, staff cottage, swimming pool, tennis court and beach access stair.

Intersecting rafters bolted to the reinforced concrete ring beam celebrate the anti-hurricane measures. The vertical sliding-folding louvered doors allow maximum openness, ventilation and enclosure as desired. The vertical bifold motion of the doors does not disrupt furniture arrangements.

The residence takes full advantage of its beautiful site, allowing for an open-air lifestyle while providing seclusion. Central to this concept are the bifold vertical doors that are located on the central living pavilion. The tropical location requires a constant breeze to provide cooling, and the slatted doors serve this purpose. The flexibility of the system allows the doors to function as both door and wall. The action of the doors prevents them from disrupting furniture and in the raised position they effectively lower the ceiling along the covered porch areas, creating a more intimate environment.

Each component of the complex is sited to take advantage of breeze, avoid wind and utilize the levels of a sloping site to advantage. Stairs and retaining walls play an important part in the connection between components and are thus given significance in the architecture.

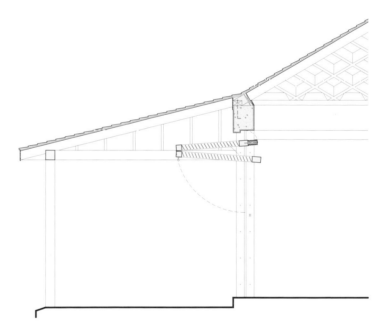

Limestone cladding with walnut window frames and bronze anodized metal detail.

Enclosed quadrangle.

LEGGATT HALL AND WATTS HALL,
QUEEN'S UNIVERSITY, KINGSTON, ONTARIO

Leggatt Hall and Watts Hall, student residences for 550 students, are designed around landscaped courts and quadrangles. Private student rooms with shared washrooms are connected in houses of six to eight suites, each with a common study and lounge space. Great halls with fireplaces form spaces for students and overlook the court and quadrangle. The buildings are clad in natural stone, continuing the university's tradition of a powerful, stone-clad built form.

The plan of Leggatt Hall illustrates open and secure quadrangles – overlooked by a common Great Hall.

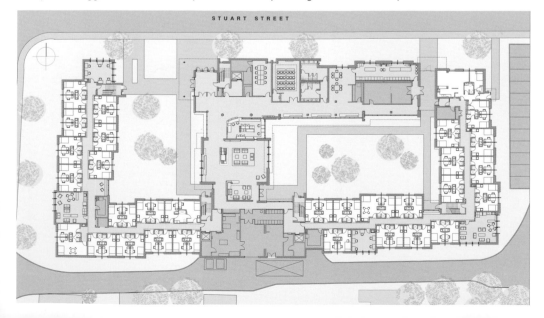

STUART STREET

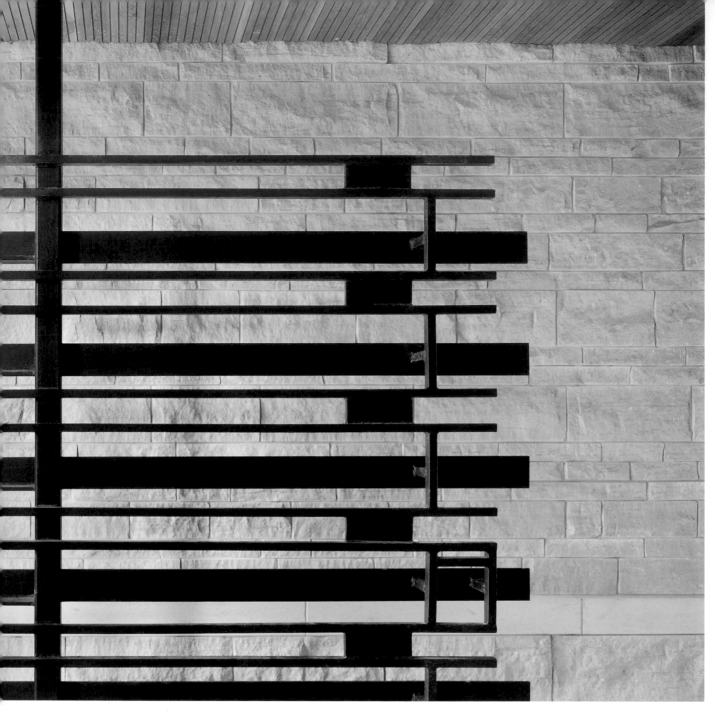

Courtyard gate.

Window detail.

Great Hall.

Ceiling detail at chimney.

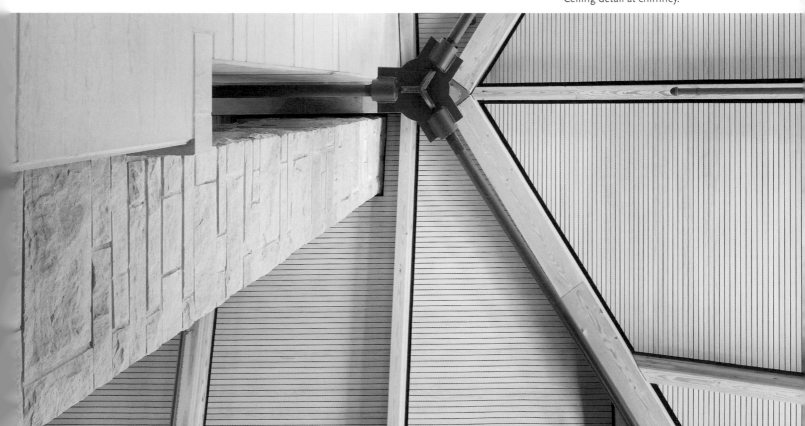

METRO CENTRAL YMCA,
TORONTO, ONTARIO

As the flagship of the YMCA in Toronto, the Metro Central YMCA continues the organization's tradition of leadership and service to inner-city residents while responding also to the lifestyle and cultural needs of the urban resident. The 14,400-square-metre building includes a comprehensive recreational complex, with two swimming pools, a double gymnasium, racquet courts, a dance studio, indoor and outdoor running tracks, a weight-training area and locker rooms. With its 300-seat flexible auditorium, 75-child daycare centre, classroom, counselling and restaurant spaces, the building caters to spirit and mind, as well as body.

The large rooms – the gymnasium, training pool, and naturally lit pool – are conceived as interior piazzette. The sports wing is connected at each level by a skylit athletes' stair, which extends from the basement to the rooftop running track. The stair provides multilevel access, brings natural light into the building and serves as an orientation devicc. Skylights over the pool and stairs bring natural light into the building and interior glass partitions provide orientation and views of the building's many activities.

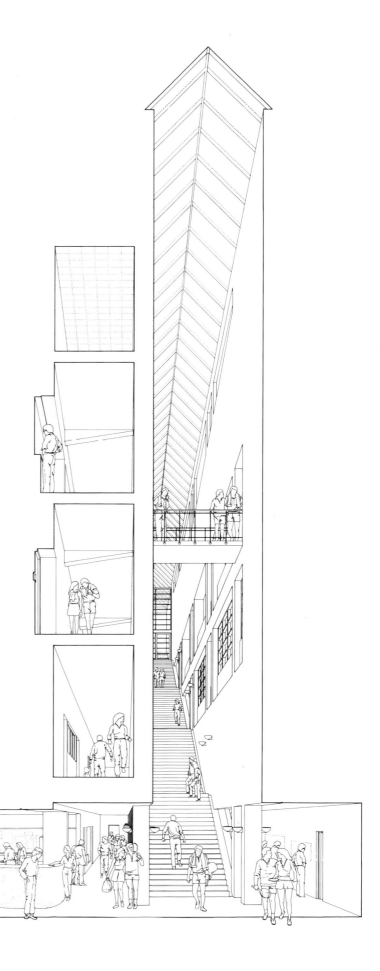

The central auditorium is at once central plaza, enclosed space, flat floor and raked theatre seating.

Ceiling coffers absorb sound and diffuse natural light, creating a tranquil pool environment.

COLLEGE RESIDENCES, LAKESHORE CAMPUS AND NORTH CAMPUS, HUMBER COLLEGE, TORONTO, ONTARIO

On the north campus of Humber College, a 290-bed student residence and conference centre opens to the adjacent arboretum landscape and is splayed on its south to shape a ravine edge. Residence rooms are paired with modest kitchen, living and washroom facilities and grouped around dining, banquet and meeting rooms open to the landscape. Clad in zinc and clay brick, the architecture sits in quiet counterpoint to the surrounding terrain.

Each floor of the south campus residence is organized around lounges and computer study areas, which appear as large, glazed exterior bays. The residence is integrated into the immediate neighbourhood, with college bookstore, café, terrace and fitness facilities on the ground floor.

Entry and projecting student commons bay window of the Lakeshore Campus Residence.

Shaped to the ravine edge, the dining room of the North Campus Residence looks south across the landscape.

MARIA SHCHUKA DISTRICT
BRANCH LIBRARY, TORONTO, ONTARIO

Providing a wide array of essential library services to a disadvantaged urban neighbourhood, this simple two-storey library is accessible, transparent and welcoming. The large bay window on the west facade brings in natural light, and the main circulation desk is located in a skylit area with a glazed stairwell connecting it to the upper floor. An open plan allows for visibility, orientation and flexible use by a broad range of constituent users.

The library establishes a powerful presence and transparent access on a major urban arterial road.

SOUTHBROOK VINEYARDS, NIAGARA-ON-THE-LAKE, ONTARIO

Southbrook Vineyards is located on a 30.35-hectare estate on a major winery route in Niagara-on-the-Lake. Central to the clients' wishes was a building that would reflect their new direction in developing high-quality wines for a discerning clientele.

The main public component of the project is a light glass pavilion juxtaposed against a 183-metre-long wall that extends across the centre of the site, parallel to the vine rows but at an angle to the main thoroughfare. The wall is a defining element of the design, marking the entry to the winery as well as the Niagara winery district. The blue wall is in contrast to the green of the vineyard or the white of winter snow, and it positions the delicate pavilion firmly in the landscape. The pavilion has two contrasting sides. From the west, the entry is defined by the only aperture in the face of the wall. From the east, the pavilion presents a more transparent facade and provides panoramic views of the vineyard.

Cross-section.

MEDICAL EDUCATION BUILDING,
UNIVERSITY OF WINDSOR, WINDSOR, ONTARIO
A small medical school designed for 48 students – this building is an addition to the Toldo Health Education Centre designed by Diamond and Schmitt in 2003. The two buildings are connected by an indoor court, which is a forum for student study and interaction. Linked with the Schulich School of Medicine at the University of Western Ontario, the school's sophisticated distance-education capability adds new technologies to virtual and real anatomy labs, clinical learning suites, simulation suites and group study rooms. Designed to LEED Gold standard, the building's south facade controls sun and view while clerestory windows admit daylight deep into the interior.

Illumination and Movement: Architecture as Kinetic Art

Man is born into light, ruled by light and even in death still seeks it.

According to the ancient Egyptians, man was born into light, ruled by light, and even in death still sought it. Designed as royal tombs, the pyramids at Giza were sheathed in white limestone to reflect the Egyptian sun. It was thought that their shape and brightness would bring the entombed closer to Ra, the sun god. In the intervening 4,000 years since the pyramids' construction, light has remained one of the most expressive elements in the architect's palette, blocking it, directing it, diffusing it, reflecting it and modulating it.

At its most prosaic level, the effective use of light can be seen in billiard rooms of a certain vintage. The often vast space is shrouded in a comforting semi-darkness, but over each table hangs a shaded light that illuminates the green felt below. The rooms themselves tend to be uneventful; the inviting aspect derives almost entirely from the lighting. The darkness agrees with pool's louche character and the intimacy defined by that rectangle of light produces a sense of refuge as well as display.

Both the quality and the quantity of natural light change with the geography. The famously warm light of Jerusalem has a specific character – a clarity and a golden glow. The *mishrabia* (latticework), pergolas and honeycomb stonework of the Jerusalem City Hall produce sharp ever-changing shadow patterns that enliven the architecture. The relentless desert light of New Mexico is, in some ways, an adversary, obscuring the view with its intensity. The brittle winter light of northern Michigan becomes a commodity to be treasured and exploited. The light is an integral part of the site, as tangible as the topography.

Light is also an inexpensive way of creating emphasis in a building. In the 1930s, German expressionist filmmakers relied on exaggerated shadow and light to heighten the drama, and even to convey story elements in their films. Their use of light in films such as *Metropolis* was creative, but it was born of necessity. They didn't have the budgets that Hollywood directors did, and they needed an inexpensive way to produce surprising and dramatic effects. The films were all shot on sound stages and relied entirely on artificial light, and this restriction was turned to advantage.

Artificial light has great character, which has been unjustly maligned by decades of crude, undifferentiated overhead fluorescent lighting that produces no shadows. The mistake most often made with artificial lighting is to use it to simulate sunlight – something it can never do. Employed economically and specifically, however, it can illuminate not just a building but also the building's themes by reinforcing either its circumstance or geometry and emphasizing the dramatic contrasts of spatial differentiation.

Light is generally democratizing. A large opaque wall invites a sense of totalitarianism, while transparency implies democracy.

Light is calibrated by structure at the University of Toronto's Bahen Centre.

UOIT Library, Oshawa: Libraries as lanterns of light in the physical and intellectual landscapes.

For buildings that often present imposing exteriors – museums, galleries, opera houses, political structures – light introduces an openness, an antidote to the sense of elitism that nags these institutions. In the day, the light comes from outside, flooding the interior, inviting scrutiny and connoting inclusion. At night, that relationship is reversed and the light inside becomes a beacon. The amount of light that is projected outwards and the quality of that light can communicate a great deal. It establishes a relationship with the city, bringing a sense of communion. During a northern winter, especially, light brings a sense of vitality, even a refuge, into the early darkness. It defines the form of the building at night and helps to delineate its presence.

Light is also an organizing element. Atria and the light they admit to a building's interior can be used to link large, dense blocks of rooms and to break up their collective mass. At the same time, atria can also be quieter, more private areas within buildings. The change in volume and light communicates a shift in purpose.

Movement and light are often aligned in architecture. People seek the light, instinctively looking for the end of the tunnel. To come into light from darkness is liberating, sometimes exhilarating. It can be used as a directional device, a way of defining pathways.

No matter how superb the photograph, still pictures of buildings can never convey the essential kinetic aspect of architecture. The approach, the passage through and the arrival at desired locations can only be appreciated by movement. Unlike sculpture, buildings are inhabited or visited and thereby impart the dynamics of movement.

Hallways are often a neglected form. With condominiums, the developers can't sell this space; and in office towers, the owners can't rent them. So from a commercial perspective they are most effective when they are narrowest. But pathways are central to the way people experience a building, from the grand hallways of Florence's Uffizi Gallery, to Frank Lloyd Wright's winding walkway in New York's Guggenheim Museum, to the generic carpeted hallway of an apartment tower.

Pathways exist not merely for logical and efficient access to a building but as places in which to meet. In creating a university master plan, for instance, there is the possibility of creating pathways that promote interaction among the diverse disciplines. It is always a challenge, though, to engineer human movement. Looking at a civic square in winter from a vantage point several storeys up, it is possible to see the paths that people make to cross the square. There is a central wide path through the snow that goes between two primary points, and lesser pathways that connect other points. People take the route that is most convenient, and one that is marked by previous travellers. But planners and architects can seduce pedestrians into certain patterns with a framed vista, or a pleasantly defined path, or a shaded or sheltered walkway.

The play of light is one of the Taj Mahal's most compelling and ingenious features, and the repetition of patterns and elements gives the impression of continuous space, of movement. The Mughal emperor Shah Jahan commissioned the Taj Mahal in 1631 as a memorial to his wife, the empress Mumtaz Mahal. Approaching the Taj Mahal, visitors initially pass through a windowless gatehouse, where their eyes dilate to adjust to the darkness. When they re-enter the brilliant Indian sunlight, the building appears in a magical haze. Viewed from across the Yamuna River on a foggy morning, the Taj Mahal seems suspended. At dusk and dawn, it radiates light. More than 350 years after its completion, the elements of movement and light retain their considerable power.

Potemkin Stairs, Odessa: Not merely stairs, but promenade, landscape, architecture, and a symbol of power.

THE ISRAELI MINISTRY OF FOREIGN AFFAIRS, JERUSALEM, ISRAEL

Located on the ceremonial National Boulevard, the Israeli Ministry of Foreign Affairs is one of a chain of buildings defining the National Precinct in Jerusalem. Within this area are the important buildings of state – the parliament buildings (Knesset), the Israel Museum and the Supreme Court.

The challenge was to provide the comprehensive security necessary for foreign delegations while at the same time conveying a sense of openness and invitation. The main reception hall has translucent walls of onyx and a roof of glass that takes advantage of Jerusalem's renowned light. Above the glass roof, a perforated metal parasol gives protection from the sun and creates dappled shadows in the room below. The mezzanine floors are also made of glass to allow the maximum penetration of light into the space. Twelve columns support the structure, and they are elegantly tapered and positioned so as not to encumber the enclosing translucent membrane. Notwithstanding the delicacy of the onyx wall, an innovative blast-resistant assembly was designed to meet the facility's need for rigorous security.

Tapered concrete columns refine the definition of the enclosure, support the mezzanine glass floors, the teak screens and, above the glass roof, the perforated metal parasol. The onyx enclosure enhances the golden light of Jerusalem within, and makes a grand lantern in the cityscape from without.

Mezzanine with glass floor.

This building has broken new ground in the use of stone for rain-screening and sun-shading purposes, and as an expressive medium.

Entrance canopy in the secure entrance car court.

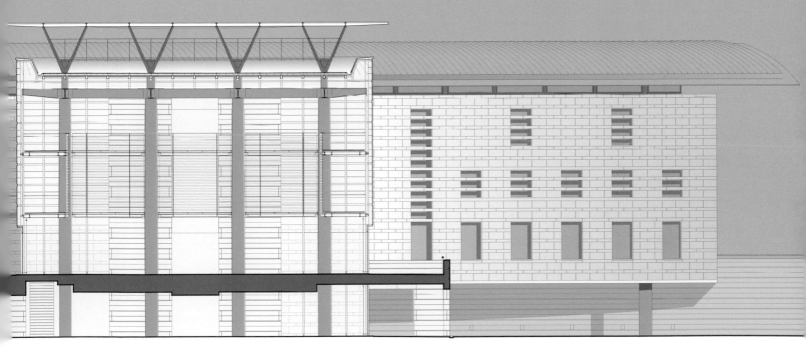

Section through the semi-submerged ballroom and roof entrance, the onyx hall above the diplomats' dining room and garden beyond.

Detail of the exterior stonework and sunshades.

The sunken ballroom is integrated into the landscape, half-buried and almost ruin-like. The roof, on which an orangerie has been situated, acts as an entrance tablum.

Stair to the foreign minister's suite.

Perforated metal parasol.

The diplomats' court.

THE APOTEX CENTRE, TORONTO, ONTARIO

Located at the Jewish Home for the Aged in the Baycrest Centre for Geriatric Care, the Apotex Centre accommodates 372 long-term-care residents and 100 beds in the Centre for Cognitive Disorders. Recognizing that a home-like environment is needed for satisfactory long-term care, the centre comprises thirty-six semi-autonomous clusters. Each one has twelve or thirteen private bedrooms and a living room, dining room and bathing room. A winter garden forms the centre of the complex, providing an all-weather gathering place. Two other protected courtyard gardens have been designed to meet the specific needs of those with Alzheimer's disease. The centre provides an environment that is attractive to residents, their families and staff, and that facilitates excellence in geriatric care, research and education.

The sunshades and high protective railings make virtues of the play of light on the solar and security protection. The juxtaposition of balconies is an essay in chiaroscuro.

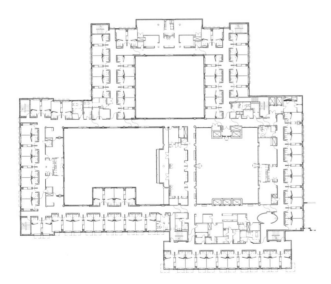

Typical floor plan.

Sunshades to the recreation room terrace.

The central atrium, with structural supports and solar shades.

The central all-weather gathering space, surrounded by
a café, recreation rooms, chapel and hairdressing salon.

PIERRE BERTON RESOURCE LIBRARY, VAUGHAN, ONTARIO

The Pierre Berton Resource Library is designed to serve the information, cultural, learning and leisure needs of a growing multicultural population. Vaughan Public Libraries has been at the forefront of mobilizing new technology to benefit library users. The new library incorporates an array of Internet-access computers, word-processing stations, and CD-ROM terminals to meet the ever-growing demand.

The facility is also designed to optimize the library's visibility in the community. The north facade along Rutherford Road is glazed, exposing all the activity inside. The double-height Internet café protrudes from this facade, and its media installation acts both as a beacon and as a source of information to library users. The ground floor is a busy area, with a children's program room and casual reading areas, while the second floor is reserved for more focused study. Quiet study rooms are available for group research. The second-floor study lounge breaks out of the main building mass, commanding a presence along Rutherford Road and providing views to the adjacent Boyd Conservation Area.

A view of the south elevation.

Second-floor study lounge.

The entry with information and circulation desks provides views and orientation to the interior.

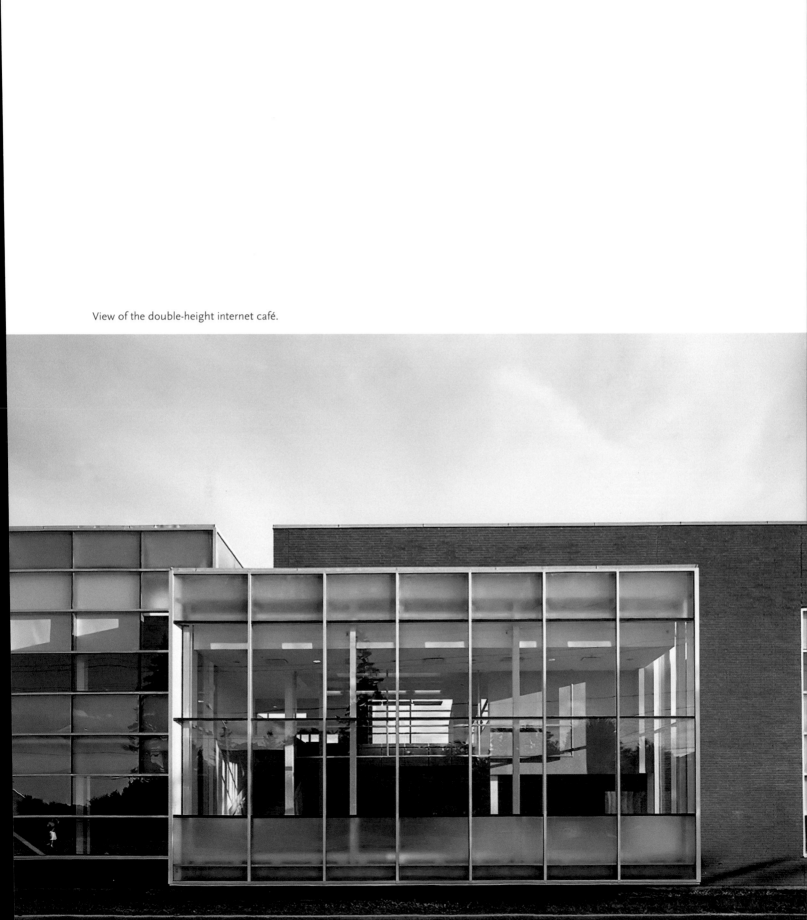

View of the double-height internet café.

ONTARIO SCIENCE CENTRE,
MASTER PLAN AND RENOVATIONS, TORONTO, ONTARIO

The Weston Family Innovation Centre encourages visitors to use their creativity and imagination and to take risks. A new master plan was commissioned for the Science Centre to plan for future changes and reviltalization. The renovation includes a new central orientation room – the Hot Zone – which provides access to three new major exhibit halls. The second component is a complete reinterpretation of the Hall of Technology, transforming it into the new Centre for Innovation and Learning. Exhibits allow visitors state-of-the-art interactivity with artists, scientists and researchers. These facilities offer an unprecedented opportunity to expand the Ontario Science Centre's visitor base, establish partnerships with various corporate and research communities, and maximize its impact on Canada's education system.

While the centre has a wide range of visitor ages, the attraction for the young is overwhelming. Here, changing light, colour and electronic images are put in the service of didactic purposes – in a sense entertainment as learning tool.

Made of structural glass and backlit with LEDs, these portals cycle through the colour spectrum while directing visitors from the Hot Zone to the exhibit halls.

THAT'S THE SAME AS 180,000 CN TOWERS!

THE SPACE ELEVATOR IS DESIGNED TO STRETCH 100,000 KM INTO SPACE.

The Hot Zone – a new central orientation room.

Built for speed.

Communication
The Living Earth
Human Body
Special Exhibitions

Communications
La Terre vivante
Le Corps humain
Expositions spéciales

Transformation of an existing wing of the building to a community-gathering place. This central feature acts as an organizing element for the campus, providing access to the principal rooms.

HOLY BLOSSOM TEMPLE, TORONTO, ONTARIO

This proposal was for a new sanctuary composed of masonry enclosing walls, relieved at the corners with glass-enveloped helical stairs. The double-glass membrane roof – one membrane above the tensile steel structure, the other below – acts as a plenum, mediating external and internal temperatures and melting any accumulating snow and ice. Supporting hollow columns supply hot and cool air to the plenum. A skein of Mylar below the roof diffuses the light and acts as a symbolic tent structure. The ark is made of black basalt set in translucent onyx, admitting light through the east facade.

Originally built in 1938, Holy Blossom Temple was the first continuously poured board-formed concrete building in Toronto – an innovation having great historical significance for both the Jewish community and the City of Toronto. In 1958, the school wing was added, expanding the temple's facilities to include nursery and day-school capabilities. The project revitalizes and expands the existing sanctuary, providing new community-oriented spaces and significantly extending the nursery and elementary school components.

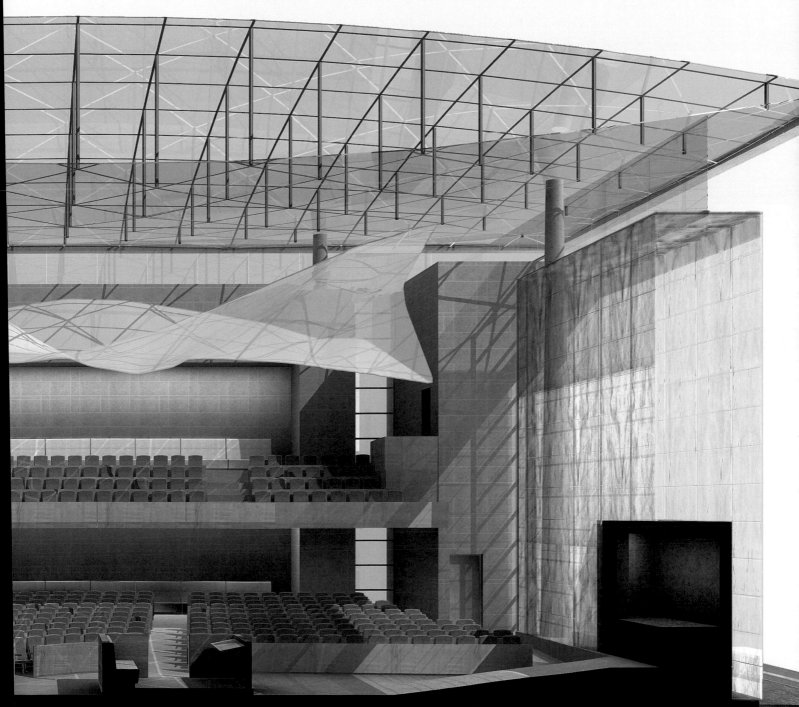

SUSUR RESTAURANT, TORONTO, ONTARIO

The architectural expression of the public spaces in this restaurant is the simplest possible, reduced to the essentials of light and space. Services are concealed, door and window casings are eliminated, baseboards are integrated into wall assemblies and hardware is concealed. To give nobility and elegance to this expression, the architectural detailing, selection of materials and the construction itself are of the highest standard, providing a neutral backdrop for the owners to display the widest possible range of art and objects.

Owing to the great care and effort with which the meals are prepared and served, diners enjoy their experience at Susur over an extended period of time. During the intervals between courses, they are entertained by diversions that stimulate their visual senses. Using dimmers and computerized controllers, two recessed rectangular wall boxes produce a slowly changing coloured glow over the course of the evening, subtly modifying the character of the dining room in the process.

As an antidote to the synthetic nature of these devices, we introduced a hyper-natural architectural feature: Two screens that separate the dining room from the lounge and corridor are made of goat vellum, which is arranged into panels and illuminated from within. The variegated texture and warm luminosity provide a feeling of comfort and luxuriousness.

Intelligent Design: Towards a Sustainable World

We are approaching a point where acts of God no longer exist. Everything will be an act of man.

In 1961, there were 3 billion people in the world, and they used approximately half the resources – food, water, arable land, energy – that the planet could sustainably provide. In 1986, there were 5 billion people, and they were using all the planet's sustainable resources. For twenty years, we have been running a deficit, exploiting forests, overfishing the oceans, filling the atmosphere with pollutants and over-fertilizing farmland to supply our needs. The forecast for 2050 is for 9 billion people, using twice the planet's resources. These figures should be frightening, but they haven't had much effect on consumption or on design. Despite what could fairly be termed a dire situation, our interests still aren't directly engaged.

One of the benefits of high energy costs is that they engage our interest. Reykjavik, Iceland, where gasoline prices are among the highest in the world, has implemented an ambitious program to use hydrogen fuel cells as a primary source of energy. North America and China, by contrast, have gas prices that are among the lowest in the world, along with massive traffic congestion and rising pollution levels. According to the World Bank, of the world's thirty most polluted cities, twenty are in China. Conservation is often a function of economics – a more powerful incentive than conscience or altruism. Even former oilman manqué George W. Bush decried America's addiction to oil. But it isn't just oil that the United States and much of the world is addicted to. As China and India move towards prosperity and a consumer culture, vast amounts of steel, aluminum and coal are also being used, as well as natural resources such as wood and water. With prosperity, come consumption, depletion and pollution.

The case for an architecture that is environmentally sustainable has never been stronger. In the relative absence of moral debate on the issue, the financial case will have to suffice. Clients are revealing a nascent willingness to explore unconventional options, if these alternatives will save them money in the longer run. The capital cost of building a sustainable structure is greater than it is for a conventional building, but it is recovered in the energy savings. In the course of a building's first twenty years, capital costs account for less than 10 per cent of the money spent on the building. More than 90 per cent of the cost goes to heating, cooling, maintenance, staff and operations. As energy costs increase, and the gap widens even further, there is a greater incentive to build energy-efficient buildings – to pay more up front and reap the benefits over the years.

Greater investment in sustainable buildings in turn spurs architects to experiment with new technologies. Sustainable design has often been viewed as a layer that is added to a building, rather than something that is integrated into the design. But fundamentally different technologies can be implemented at the design stage.

Geothermal heating systems represent a non-polluting way to reduce heating and cooling demands for residential, commercial and institutional buildings. The new University of Ontario Institute of Technology harvests this thermal energy from the earth – using wells that are 183 metres deep. The wells reject heat in the summer and recover it in the winter. The energy savings from geothermal technology are augmented by a heat-recovery system that recycles the heat generated by computers, lights and people to heat the campus buildings. The energy costs are significantly less than for conventional systems, and they are more static and predictable, and therefore more easily budgeted for, than the volatile price of natural gas.

The UOIT campus is a model for a new sustainable society. Borehole technology significantly decreases greenhouse gas emissions. Under the Kyoto Accord, Canada was supposed to reduce its carbon emissions by 6 per cent. Instead, it increased them by 24 per cent. In the United States, the situation is worse, and a thirty-year trend towards improvement has been reversed, with both water and air becoming dirtier. Most governments have been unable to address this problem with any conviction, and there is inadequate initiative in the private sector.

In Iceland, geothermal heat is used in 87 per cent of the country's homes and buildings. Hydroelectric dams and the geothermal network have replaced oil as the dominant source of power, and the country plans to be completely oil-free by 2050. But this kind of concerted, integrated approach from government is unlikely to happen in North America in the next few years, if ever. In the meantime, architects can pursue private initiatives.

The roofs at UOIT are planted with vegetation to help keep unwanted solar energy from heating the building, reduce the negative effects caused by heat islands, and aid in the absorption of rainwater. They also improve the air quality inside the buildings, as the intake comes from the cooler, cleaner, vegetated surface of the roof. But this source also raises the dismal debate on which is less safe – the outside atmosphere, with its mixture of greenhouse gases, benzene, and particulates, or inside air, with its volatile organic compounds emitted by carpets, glue, paint, and plastics. The former is responsible for the alarming rise in asthma and respiratory disease – again China is leading the way, with 400,000 premature deaths attributed annually to air pollution. This pollution is responsible for sore eyes, headaches, fatigue, and, ultimately, lost productivity.

As a way of dealing with toxic interior air, a bio-filter – a living wall of tropical plants that includes orchids and bromeliads – is surprisingly effective. It can filter about 70 per cent of a building's air. The bio-filter wall was developed at the University of Guelph-Humber. It both improves the air quality and reduces the air-conditioning load and energy consumption. The theoretical idea of a bio-wall initially prompted inquiries from clients about maintenance, insects, cost efficiencies and water issues. But after its successful implementation, others have come to want it.

The integrated approach to sustainable design at UOIT extends to the treatment of stormwater, which is traditionally collected in catch basins, piped to sewers and then moved to treatment plants. The water is returned directly to the soil to recharge the groundwater. Heavy rains are collected in storm catchment ponds. Specified plants are cultivated to act as bio-filters, cleaning out pollutants and releasing clean water into lakes or rivers.

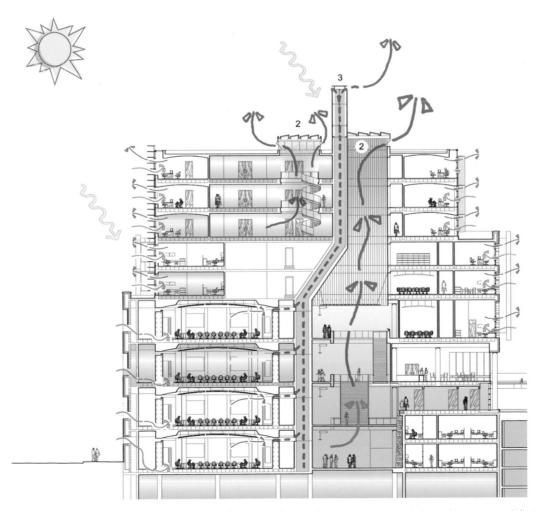

Glass chimneys, superheated by the sun, induce natural ventilation in the proposed design of the ten-storey Bank Street Senate Office Building on Parliament Hill, Ottawa.

University of Ontario Institute of Technology: Storm water in the parking areas is directed through a series of vegetated bio-swales, which pre-filter the water before it is routed to the storm-water management pond. The bio-swales allow for some infiltration and ground water recharge and reduce the heat island effect of the asphalt paving.

Two significant obstacles to sustainable design are the construction industry, which can be inflexible and entrenched in its technologies and commercial development interests, which, with exceptions, tend to be short-sighted. Each one views sustainable design not as an opportunity but as an expensive and punitive imposition. The UOIT campus demonstrates otherwise.

Currently, the predominant structure being built in North America is the single-family home, erected in the expanding suburbs and using standardized designs that are cheaply built. The benefits are purely for the builder; the occupant inherits all the energy inefficiencies.

In the urban core, developers use glass as their main external material when they construct condominiums. It is a relatively cheap way to build, and it is a primary marketing tool when selling the view. But the various sides of the buildings are not differentiated, so that the southern and western sides, where the heat gain is acute, use the same design and materials as the shaded north and east sides. The cost of heating and cooling this inefficient plan is passed on to the buyer. When buyers are given the choice, however, some will choose energy efficiency, paying more initially to reap future savings.

With governments reluctant to take environmental initiatives, and private industry not interested, the consumer has been leading the way. Change has come in response to consumption patterns. But to rely on the marketplace to solve environmental problems is a dangerous strategy. A Pew Research Center poll in the United States showed that 41 per cent of Americans still considered environmental activists to be "extremists."

Architecture that addresses energy and resource issues at the design stage has become a necessity. We can no longer afford to build wasteful monuments that gratify commercial interests or the sponsors of extravagant institutional and public buildings, all at the expense of the larger good. The climate is being destabilized, oceans are rebelling, the atmosphere is toxic and we are consuming materials at an unprecedented rate. We are approaching a point, paleontologist Tim Flannery has warned, where acts of God no longer exist. Everything will be an act of man.

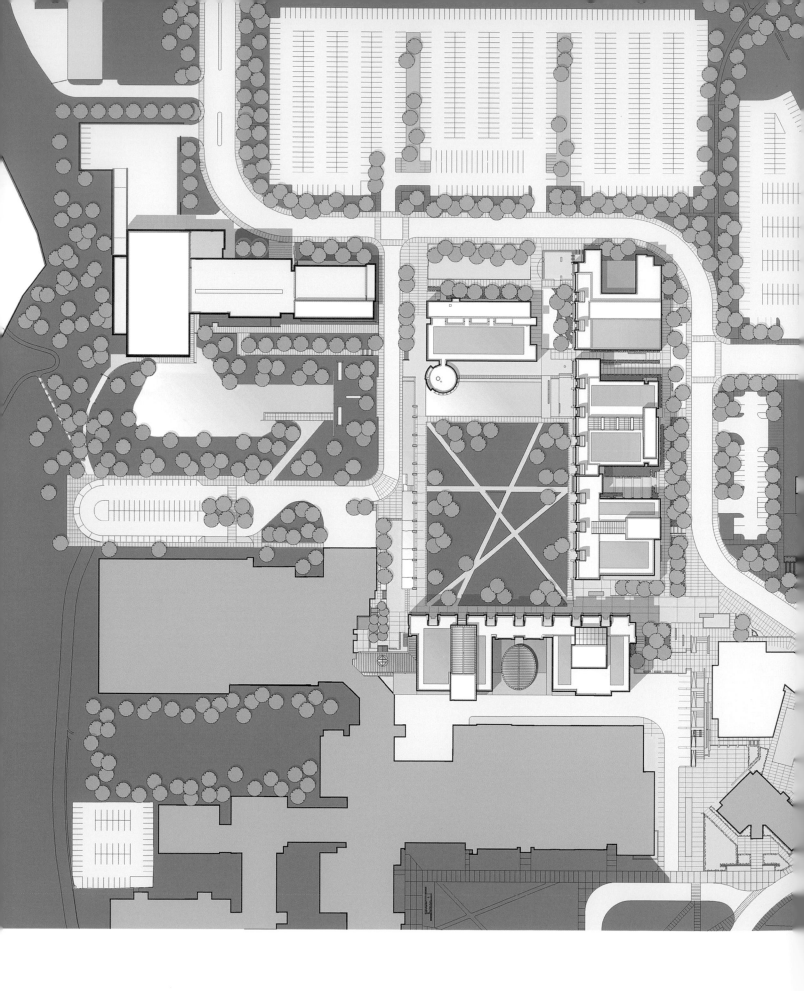

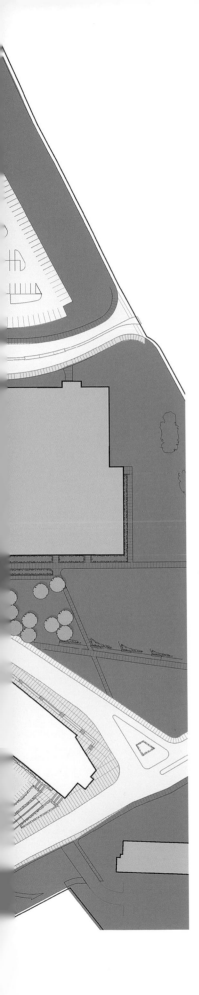

UNIVERSITY OF ONTARIO INSTITUTE OF TECHNOLOGY – CAMPUS AND BUILDINGS, OSHAWA, ONTARIO

For the first new university campus in Ontario in thirty-five years, the architects were presented with the rare opportunity to create an innovative and sustainable academic community on a large and integrated scale. The heart of the campus is a landscaped commons surrounded by five academic buildings and the University Library. While each academic building establishes separate identity and access from the perimeter ring road, a connected collegial pedestrian precinct is established around the green campus commons.

Located beneath the commons is a Borehole Thermal Energy Storage System (BTESS) that harvests energy stored in the earth for heating in the winter and cooling in the summer. The system comprises 392 closed-loop boreholes that extend 190 metres below the surface of the commons and provide 2,000 tons of energy-efficient sustainable heating and cooling.

A comprehensive water management strategy, including rainwater collection and a retention pond, was employed to protect an adjacent watershed. Green roofs assist in keeping unwanted solar energy from heating the buildings, reduce the negative effects of heat islands, and help to consume rainwater. Materials have been selected for their durability, recycled content and effect on indoor air. A key feature of the buildings is their exposed concrete structure, which allows the mass of the concrete to store and moderate thermal energy, resulting in greater comfort while also contributing to lower energy demands.

The collection, cleaning and release of stormwater into the Oshawa Creek watershed is celebrated with reflecting pool and skating rink, linear wetland and new pond.

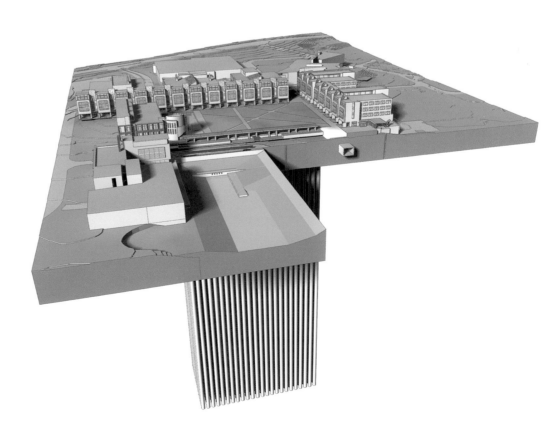

Clusters of faculty offices separated by seminar and student study rooms enclose the campus commons. Continuous colonnades provide weather-protected connection between academic disciplines.

Each academic discipline and building is planned around an interior winter garden, each of different character, serving as places of connection and interaction.

Copper, clay brick, cedar, limestone and glass are the palette of the academic village.

This colonnade provides weather-protected connection between academic disciplines, frames the great outdoor room of the campus commons and is a belvedere framing distant views of wild conservation lands to the west.

The interior court of the new Engineering Building brings light and access deep into the interior.

A new Student Center and Classroom Building connects the campus common to the University Gateway on Simcoe Street, thus connecting town and gown.

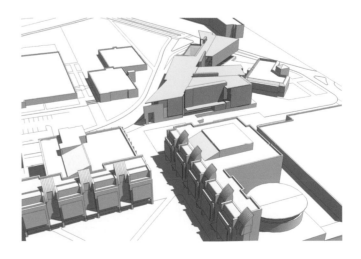

UNIVERSITY OF GUELPH-HUMBER, TORONTO, ONTARIO

Designed to a budget of 10 per cent less than conventional academic buildings, a simple plan organizes all academic spaces around a four-storey skylit interior court.

This strategy reduces circulation area but ensures interaction between students and faculty. The crossroads of the court is further reinforced by a sculptural stair connecting all floors and a series of balconies at all levels, which accommodates casual gatherings or informal group study. The acoustics of the court were carefully designed to support gregarious gathering and to allow intimate conversation to occur simultaneously.

The court, open to all floors, was designed as a return air plenum for 40 per cent of the building, using displacement ventilation, which is filtered through a living bio-filter wall, increasing indoor air quality by 50 per cent and reducing energy consumption by as much as 35 per cent.

The 60- and 120-seat classrooms, library, teaching spaces, and offices circle the court, which combines sustainable architecture with a collegial and comfortable academic environment.

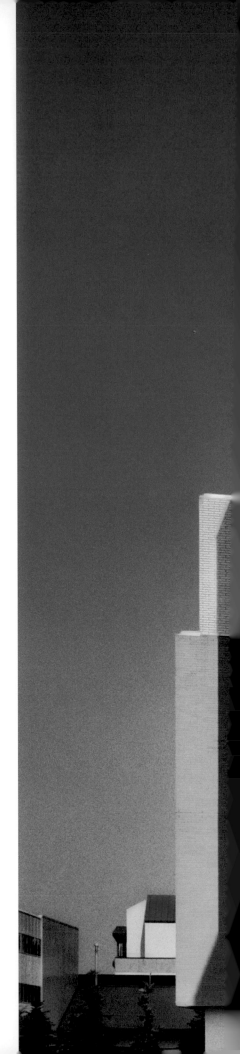

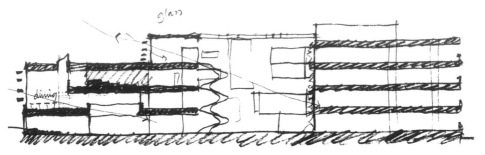

An interior sunlight court lies at the centre of this 14,000-square-metre academic building. Circled by all teaching, library, office and café spaces, the court provides places for informal gathering, study and encounter. Carefully designed acoustics allow for quiet communication.

A spiral stair constructed in concrete reinforces the court as an academic crossroads.

A living bio-filter wall improves air quality by 50 per cent and reduces fan energy consumption by as much as 30 per cent.

EVERGREEN AT THE BRICK WORKS, TORONTO, ONTARIO

Diamond and Schmitt Architects are part of a team shaping the adaptive reuse and revitalization of the Don Valley Brick Works Factory, a derelict industrial site in the heart of Toronto's ravine system. The Evergreen Foundation is creating Canada's first full-fledged, large-scale environmental discovery centre in the project. The existing buildings are renovated to retain heritage character and to introduce sustainability. The Welcome Centre and Administration Building, the only new building on the site, provides community office space and serves as a showcase for green design. The design knits the new building into existing elements while creating a prominent place for community expression. A track system allows changing movable screens, window boxes and large art installations to animate the building facade. Thus the facade acts as a canvas for the Evergreen community. The flexible exterior skin brings together nature, culture and community.

The Evergreen Brick Works complex serves as an incubator and laboratory for sustainable design ideas and techniques and this building is designed to achieve LEED (Leadership in Energy and Environmental Design) Platinum certification. Numerous sustainable features have been incorporated into the building's design, including green roofs and a bio-filter plant wall. The south side of the building features a breathing/solar wall, that uses the sun to pre-warm fresh air before it enters the building, resulting in significant energy savings. On the east facade a vertical wetland has been incorporated as part of the stormwater management system. These wetlands filter rainwater for use as irrigation in the gardens. The Welcome Centre and Administration Building is also integrated into a geothermal system that serves all the Brick Works facilities.

CENTRE FOR ADVANCED MANUFACTURING AND DESIGN TECHNOLOGIES
SHERIDAN COLLEGE, BRAMPTON, ONTARIO

The Centre for Advanced Manufacturing and Design Technologies is the first building in Canada to fully integrate a system of thermal storage and air delivery in the precast concrete plank floor. The system offers significant energy savings and enhanced comfort by using the thermal mass of standard hollow-core precast concrete slabs in an economical and speedy construction process. The system uses 100 per cent fresh air, and the energy is radiated or absorbed by the concrete slabs rather than through air movement. Branch ductwork is virtually eliminated, resulting in cleaner lines, better acoustics and teaching spaces.

Other sustainable strategies include the use of a ductless air supply in the gymnasium, thereby reducing the gross weight of metal in the project. The long trusses in the gym are combined with cable bottom chord and wood-plank decking – a process that vastly reduces the use of steel in the building. A customized curtain-wall mullion and an airfoil aluminum sunshade system protect the south facade from heat gain.

Gymnasium steel trusses.

A customized mullion and sunshade system animates the monumental
south facade and protects it from heat gain.

The atrium.

206

LIFE SCIENCES CENTRE, UNIVERSITY OF BRITISH COLUMBIA, VANCOUVER, BRITISH COLUMBIA

The 52,000-square-metre Life Sciences Centre is the hub of a network of teaching and research facilities that focus on health education, medical training, and research, including anatomy, biochemistry, molecular biology, cell biology, medical genetics and bio-informatics. Flexible wet and dry research laboratory modules and associated support spaces are distributed along three wings, each five-storeys high and connected by two atria. The flexibility was delivered via the structural and mechanical systems: a simple repetitive structural grid and clear permanent trunk infrastructure with flexible branches. The trunk lines lie along the circulation and preparation-room spine, with the flexible components in the laboratory ceiling.

Walls to the atrium, not being external walls, were able to be economically constructed. Lined with wood slats screening a sound-absorbent substratum, the atrium is a quiet place for study or leisure. Large windows were also thus made possible, providing ample light for the laboratories.

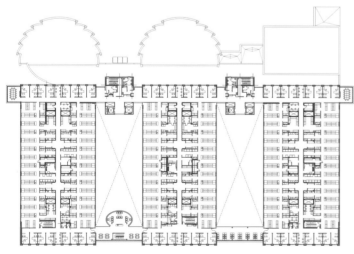

The major lecture theatres are provided with natural light and advanced electronic audio-visual systems for distance learning. In this case it is possible to interconnect all of the major health-care facilities in British Columbia.

The laboratories are enclosed by researchers' offices at upper levels, with the major lecture halls at grade.

The repetitive structure, mechanical and electrical systems made possible the modular laboratories (shown here prior to occupation). This arrangement allows changes to laboratory size and the reconfiguration of services to be made with minimal disruption.

At the ground floor, the large auditoria, classrooms and specialized teaching spaces front the main east/west colonnade. The east atrium contains a café and food services and is used as an informal assembly hall. The west atrium includes study tables and modulated lighting to create a quiet reading room. The basement floor accommodates more secure service areas, including mechanical and electrical rooms, loading dock facilities, some core support laboratory space, the bio-level 3 laboratory and animal care facility, a morgue and gross anatomy teaching spaces. All above-ground spaces receive natural light.

INDIGO RESIDENCE, MUSTIQUE, THE GRENADINES

The Indigo Residence is a family vacation villa located on the Caribbean island of Mustique in the West Indies. Situated on 2.8 hectares of sloping hillside overlooking the Atlantic Ocean, the villa comprises 112 square metres of open-air spaces and 200 square metres of enclosed space, including the main family quarters and separate houses for guests and staff. The complex has a swimming pool and terrace, a reflecting-pool courtyard, walled garden courts, sunbathing and showering patios, indoor and outdoor dining areas and a rooftop terrace.

Below-ground cisterns with a storage capacity of 455 cubic metres collect rainwater runoff, and the villa is equipped with a water purification system, an onsite irrigation network and a self-contained domestic wastewater treatment plant. A rooftop solar-energy collection system offsets water-heating costs, and energy-efficient appliances and lighting systems are used throughout the complex. In addition, natural ventilation is maximized along with selected zone air conditioning.

Set on a site that is subject to strong and persistent wind, considerations of the local climate and conditions were paramount in the design and construction of the project. Durable local and traditional building finishes such as plaster, painted wood and floor tile were incorporated into the villa's design, as were hurricane- and termite-resistant construction techniques.

The simplicity of the colonnaded verandahs, the location of the openings and courtyard, the calmness of the water court and the strictly limited palette of materials used throughout, create a house that is a cool haven in a tough tropical environment.

Life in Old Structures: Renovation and Reuse

Society came late to the concept of recycling — perhaps too late.

In the 1980s, news footage of garbage barges moving from port to port, their increasingly offensive cargo repeatedly refused, provided a bleak image of the future. We were faced with the concrete evidence of what a day's waste from a city looked like. What to do with all that garbage? Incineration contributes to air pollution, while landfills present the dangers of mercury and hazardous chemicals leaching into the earth. Here was a graphic illustration of the disposable economy.

Society came late to the concept of reuse – perhaps too late. The earliest and most vocal opponents of recycling were, not surprisingly, waste-management companies: They argued that recycling was expensive and that a viable market for recycled materials didn't exist. Commercial interests have used comparable arguments to explain their reluctance to recycle buildings. The owners of old buildings often say they are too costly to maintain and too expensive to renovate. So they are torn down and replaced by expedient, profitable constructions of indifferent design quality, using material with a limited lifespan, making them ultimately disposable.

But the cost of renovating can be less than the cost of demolition and new construction, especially if the embodied energy and disposal costs are factored in. Often it is only the initial costs that are calculated. There are other advantages to retaining historic buildings. Recycled structures help to retain memory and community, provide an aesthetic continuity, preserve craftsmanship or architectural detail we can no longer afford and minimize environmental waste. Revitalization of old buildings creates an enriched and more complex city fabric.

Buildings decay at a prescribed rate. The surface elements are the first to go: paint, floor coverings, perhaps the roofing, followed by the electrical and mechanical systems. The decision to raze a building is sometimes made on these superficial grounds; it looks like hell. But, typically, the structure is the most resilient aspect, capable of supporting a new life. In the core of most cities are century-old buildings whose beauty has faded, but whose construction remains robust and flexible. Built before the advent of an electrical grid, many old factories, warehouses and churches have large windows to let in natural light, high ceilings and solid concrete, brick and wood frames that were designed to support heavy industrial machinery. Once the building is determined to be structurally sound, the next question is merely one of imagination. The deconsecrated church can be reconfigured into condominiums, the garment factory turned into art galleries and photography studios, the derelict generating station converted to a film studio, the antiquated pumphouse made into a theatre.

The argument for recycling presupposes the existence of old buildings, which are endangered in many cities. They disappear for different reasons. In Montreal, the Square Mile once housed the nineteenth-century merchant class. From the lower slopes of Mount Royal down to Boulevard René Lévesque, there were eclectic mansions that incorporated Gothic, Tudor, Italianate and Victorian features designed to fulfill their owners' sense of New World royalty. The business class was both arrogant and insecure, and entrepreneurs used architecture as a way of establishing status and identity. But by the early twentieth century, most of the houses were too large for the smaller families and too expensive for what in many cases had become smaller fortunes. Some of these mansions were adapted as hospital or university buildings or remade into foreign embassies. In 1953, high-rise apartments were zoned into the Square Mile and the remaining Edwardians suddenly had a hundred balconies staring down into their world. The vast majority of the houses were razed. Today, less than a quarter of the original greystone mansions have survived in any form.

Local economies play a large part in the fate of old buildings. Winnipeg's comparatively stagnant economy has been a boon for preservation. The city has one of the best collections of turn-of-the-century bank and office buildings on the continent because there wasn't the pressure to raze them to make way for new developments. Today they are being reconfigured into multipurpose buildings that combine retail, residential and office space.

Calgary, by contrast, with its overheated oil economy, has always been quick to discard the old and build something new. In the early 1980s and again in the early twenty-first century, the city experienced periods of extraordinary growth fuelled by rising oil prices. In 1981, Calgary issued $2.5 billion in building permits, more than Chicago or New York. Buildings were being taken down with great haste and efficiency to make room for a commercial downtown core. The impetus to conserve was anathema to both an economy and a spirit based on growth and consumption.

In 1980, the Burns Building in downtown Calgary, a classical Edwardian structure built in 1913, was slated for demolition because it was on land promised for the Calgary Centre for the Performing Arts. The building, partially clad in cream-coloured terra cotta, was important historically, architecturally and culturally. Patrick Burns had been a hugely successful meat packer, as well as one of the founders of the Calgary Stampede, and this structure served as headquarters for the family's meat business. It also helped to preserve a human scale in the downtown centre, which was quickly being transformed by high-rises of indifferent

The Burns Building, Calgary: Threatened with demolition, this former headquarters of the Burns Meat Packing Company was given new life for office, retail, and restaurant uses.

quality. The strong opposition to the demolition led to DSAI being commissioned to design a reconfigured plan that incorporated the Burns Building into what is today known as the EPCOR Centre for the Performing Arts. The reuse of the structure was a victory on several counts and, even more significant at the time, its retention demonstrated that recycling was economically viable, that it could be done.

Recycling a building requires more than just a philosophical predisposition. You need political will, which is often in short supply. The deregulation of civic zoning laws allows for mixed use, combining residential, commercial, service and retail, which makes the buildings more viable economically. The combined benefits of revitalized old structures and the integration of mixed-use buildings into a neighbourhood can be profound. There is increased interaction and a sense of civic place and belonging that gives life to the street – and that in turn fosters growth. It is an effective tool in maintaining or creating a viable downtown core.

For years, the centres of North American cities presented a dialectic that pitted human scale against commerce. As one mayor stated in the 1980s, "In our efforts to make the commercial core a more human place, we must be careful to avoid the trap of putting sunlight ahead of commerce. Sunlight does not turn the wheels of our factory." As a result, the downtown core resembled a factory in many ways; it emptied at the end of the day as workers returned to the suburbs, leaving an inhospitable shell. But sunlight, along with parks, residential structures and cultural activities that keep people downtown after business hours, helps to turn the wheels of the factory. A city's competitive advantage depends on several factors, chief among them quality of life. The desire to build new structures, combined with the reluctance to recycle, has contributed to economic stagnation and subsequent competitive decline.

To "unslum" a slum, to use Jane Jacobs' terminology, it is not enough to keep people from leaving. If they dream of leaving, it is enough to undermine reclamation, because their efforts are going towards escape rather than improvement. One of the benefits of converting existing buildings is that it creates a sense of revitalization, of possibility. Demolition implies there is nothing of value there. When designing new spaces, we should consider that demographics will shift, that economies will fluctuate and evolve, and our structures must be capable of accommodating these changes.

Berkeley Castle (above right) is a mixed-use retail and office complex, incorporating a group of industrial buildings located in Toronto's St. Lawrence neighbourhood. The five buildings (above left) originally housed the city's first knitting mill and had been condemned by the fire marshal at the time of the renovation.

The Great Hall, Ontario Science Centre. The architectural infrastructure was renovated to clarify the orientation for visitors, identifying the route to the exhibit halls. Unused escalators were removed, allowing additional windows and natural light to flood the space. A rotating David Rockeby art installation, *Cloud*, hangs from the ceiling, creating an iconic focal point while still allowing floor space to be used for temporary exhibits and events.

BETTY OLIPHANT THEATRE,
CANADA'S NATIONAL BALLET SCHOOL,
TORONTO, ONTARIO

The Betty Oliphant Theatre provides a stage training facility for the National Ballet School in downtown Toronto. Until recently, the school occupied a number of smaller buildings near the site. The stage-training centre and theatre provide a focal point that ties together the different properties as a campus. The stage-training centre sits on a compact site incorporating two Victorian houses of historical and architectural importance, and the houses were renovated to provide an elegant formal entrance to both the theatre and the ballet campus. Their relationship to the street is unaltered and provides effective screening of the stage-house bulk.

The Betty Oliphant Theatre is a small, technically sophisticated theatre with a stage comparable in size and equipment to major North American performance spaces. The intent was to create a professional performance environment for training students. Auditorium seating for 300 is fully retractable and when stored creates a large dance studio for daily classes.

The fly tower to the theatre is grafted on behind the restored nineteenth-century houses, converted to front-of-house facilities and teaching space. The house mitigates the change of scale introduced by the tall fly tower.

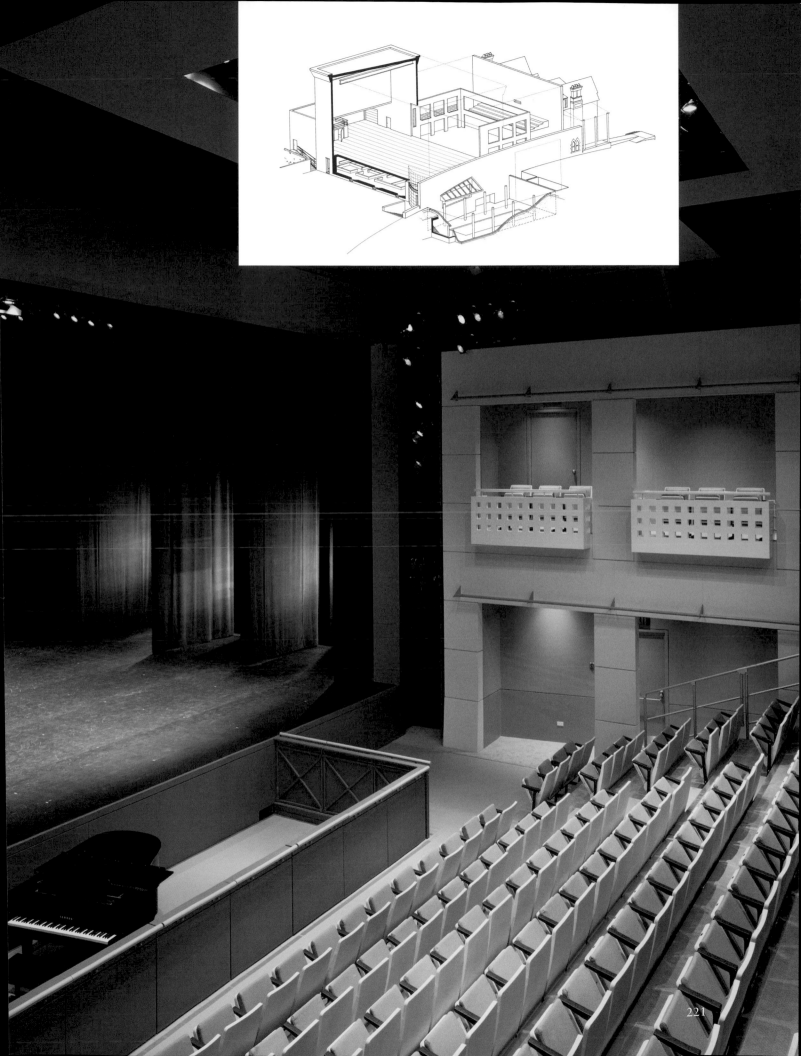

The aperture between ground and second floors provides views of the film and other visitor-information facilities above.

CAPITAL INFORMATION CENTRE, OTTAWA, ONTARIO

An existing heritage building was renovated to provide interpretation and orientation to the national capital, Ottawa. A new entrance and second-level bay window were introduced on a flanking party wall facing Parliament Hill, the House of Commons and Senate. A new exterior court provides space for exterior programs, gathering and celebration. A proposed tilted granite relief map of Canada provides visitors with a connection to the country and its topography. The information centre provides connection to events and landmarks in the capital.

Exposed by the demolition of the adjacent building, the party wall now features a viewing gallery of Parliament Hill.

A perspective view of the proposed forecourt design facing the Parliament buildings.

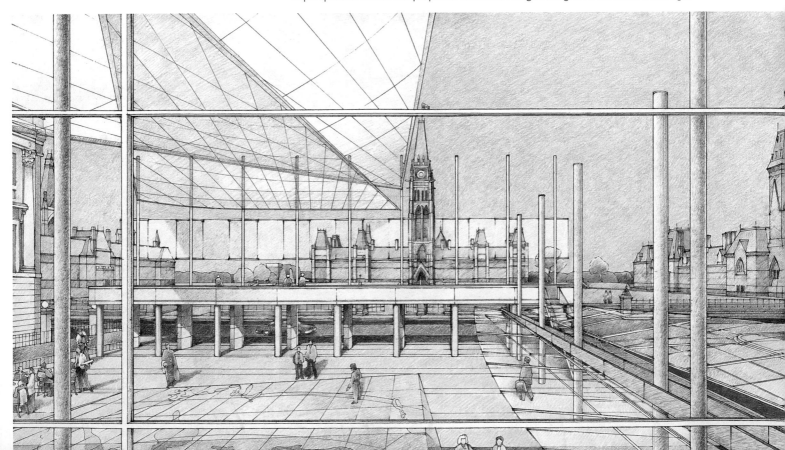

Exterior view.

CANADIAN CHANCERY, PRAGUE, CZECH REPUBLIC

Even though the facade of the Jugendstil building was intact, the interior had been poorly renovated by a large commercial company. To make the structure suitable to serve as an embassy, the interior was gutted and a stable structure was again put in place. A welcoming entrance, consistent with Canada's open democracy, was created, and the renovation now provides secure and comfortable accommodation for Canadian diplomats and the consular services they provide.

BERKELEY CASTLE, TORONTO, ONTARIO

Located in Toronto's St. Lawrence neighbourhood, the rehabilitation of a group of industrial buildings yielded a mixed-use retail and office complex. These five buildings originally housed Toronto's first knitting mill, and they had been condemned at the time of renovation. The first of them, built in 1868, was once on the waterfront, and newer buildings were added over time in an ad hoc manner as landfill created more lake frontage and the mill expanded. The restoration involved extensive rebuilding and renovation to bring the buildings up to contemporary standards. At the heart of the complex is a courtyard that was created by demolishing one of the structures. Diamond and Schmitt Architects' offices were located in this complex for more than twenty years.

LEGISLATIVE ASSEMBLY OF ONTARIO – RENOVATION MASTER PLAN AND IMPLEMENTATION, TORONTO, ONTARIO

Since 1993, when the firm prepared a renovation and restoration master plan for the interior of this public landmark, first constructed in 1893, Diamond and Schmitt have served as restoration architects for the implementation of the plan conducted in many phases.

The complete interior renovation and restoration of the 42,000-square-metre Legislative Assembly of Ontario building was intended to accommodate the requirements for a public ceremonial and office building in the twenty-first century. The project included a full upgrade of the security, mechanical, electrical, data communications, fire and life-safety systems. The restoration of the interior continues to be undertaken to the highest conservation standards.

The firm recognized the need for sympathetic interior design elements, based on heritage research, along with climatic controls to preserve and protect heritage artworks. Restored areas throughout the legislative building are intended to be more accessible to the visiting public.

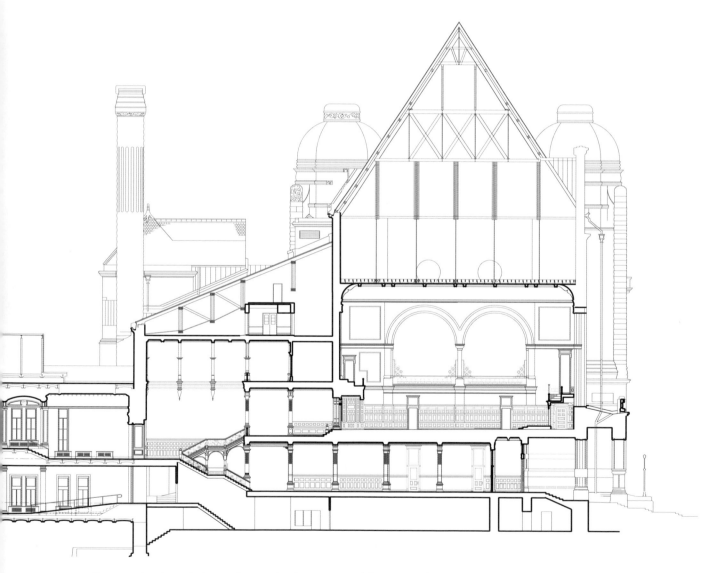

Cross-section through the south entry, the Great Stair and the House of Commons.

Waste Not: Economy of Means

What begins as a bold statement can descend into advertisement — though it isn't always clear what is being advertised.

Designed by the French architect Roger Taillibert for the 1976 Olympic Games, Montreal's Olympic Stadium was the architectural centrepiece of the event. The most notable feature of the stadium's design – a giant retractable Kevlar roof, to be manoeuvred by a 160-metre tower – wasn't ready for the opening, and the project went well over budget. Still, the stadium was a grand statement, one that spoke to Olympic ambition. Little more than a decade later, however, the building lay largely deserted, the roof remained inoperative and large chunks of concrete were falling from the stadium. The structure was held together with makeshift bolts that gave it the look of Frankenstein; the original budget of $120 million had ballooned to $1.3 billion. The resources that went into the Olympic Stadium were epic, but ultimately the structure was not. It was functionally impoverished and in the end financially crushing.

The Olympic Stadium now stands as a symbol of failure and excess. The failure was the mammoth gap between the building's design and the demands of gravity. On paper, the simple graphic pencil lines of Taillibert's plan for the stadium had a certain grace. The architect's elegant sketch was given to the building's engineers, who grappled unsuccessfully with its challenges. The idea of the architect as master builder had given way entirely to the idea of the architect as artist.

For centuries, architects were conversant with the details of construction and the limits of engineering. The Santa Maria del Fiore cathedral in Florence took 140 years to build, requiring a technology that still has an element of mystery almost six centuries later. The cathedral's hemispherical roof remains perhaps the highest and widest masonry dome ever constructed, and its architect, Filippo Brunelleschi, faced some of the same hurdles as the engineers of Montreal's Olympic Stadium. But with Santa Maria del Fiore, the building's architecture and its engineering were intrinsically joined; despite the scale and opulence of the cathedral, there was an economy of means in its construction. The building was made using local materials, including marble from nearby Carrara, and Brunelleschi himself designed some of the machines and tools necessary to build the dome.

On a more modest scale, the adobe buildings of New Mexico are also an example of economy of means. These indigenous vernacular dwellings are constructed from local materials and their thick clay walls keep the heat out during the day, storing the warmth and radiating it during the cool nights. Adobes are cost- and energy-efficient, a logical response to the desert environment in the same way that an igloo, in both shape and material, is the logical response to the Arctic.

But urban buildings don't often adhere to logic or an economy of means. Modernism brought buildings that were stripped to their essence; an aesthetic and structural economy. Mies van der Rohe's skyscrapers were beautifully proportioned and they projected a sense of restraint and elegance – though their symmetric form didn't acknowledge the asymmetry of heat load and loss. The development industry quickly seized on the economical aspect of Mies' work, but often ignored its elegance. The form of his skyscrapers was repeated in ever-diminishing versions, resulting in cities that are filled with listless high-rises: They represent a certain economy, but lack imagination, balance and proportion.

The postmodern response to this commercial architecture, with its ironic decoration and detail, brought neither clarity nor beauty. Although it began like most movements with a burst of energy, many of its buildings soon become tired-looking, even cartoonish. Perhaps that is why the exuberant sculptural forms of subsequent years have been received with such enthusiasm.

Today, the current trend of iconic sculptural architecture is showing signs of flagging. Iconic architecture is usually viewed as an individualistic statement, and by extension a blow against faceless corporate tyranny. But the imposition of a purely aesthetic form on the needs and movements of people is really corporate control under the guise of liberation. When a building's facade is given more importance than its function, idiosyncratic design may leave users with fewer actual choices: control over heating and cooling, for example, or access to natural light. It may come with unwieldy challenges – non-perpendicular walls and eccentric spaces in a museum, for instance, that are the bane of exhibit designers struggling to mount a show.

Light structure on an elevated stick platform, to gather breeze for cooling in hot humid climates that have small daily changes in temperature.

Adobe housing. The empirical adaptation to circumstance with limited means: thick walls to warm slowly through the hot desert day and cool slowly through the cold desert night. Small windows as protection from the desert glare – windows as irises of architecture.

The trend towards iconic architecture arrived at an unfortunate moment. Just as we were seeing the depletion of available resources, an architecture that uses an excess of material and money came into vogue. As building and design technologies evolve and as urbanism demands new forms, there has been greater emphasis on technological progress and less on the economy of means. Calculations that would have taken months previously can now be done in a matter of hours with computers, so engineering that once would have been impossible is now almost routine. Instead of using these powerful tools to reduce structures to their minimum, they are used to prop up forms conceived in the abstract. Frequently, even more effort and a greater variety of materials are used in support of the design. Exotic materials can be shipped across the world and machined into any shape or thickness or configuration. Although there are obvious advantages to these technological innovations, there are insidious drawbacks as well. Design shortcomings can be masked or compensated for more easily. In the human body, pain is a defense mechanism: When you feel it, you withdraw. In architecture, however, there is an unwarranted sense of immunity, and architects have become adept at disguising a building's pain. To use this sophisticated technology to produce unhealthy, wasteful structures is a perversion of purpose.

Starting with a building's function, the architect should ask what technology will most efficiently accommodate the users, what form will best express that purpose and what materials will celebrate it.

Diamond and Schmitt's Bahen Centre for Information Technology at the University of Toronto is a cross-disciplinary teaching and research centre that required flexibility in its program and configuration. It is energy-efficient (warm and cool air are delivered by a low-velocity distribution system that results in significant savings in the amount of sheet metal needed for ductwork, the size of the fan needed to push the air and the energy consumption of that fan), and allows users to choose their own climate. In its materials and massing, the brick and glazed exterior reflects both its high-tech purpose and its relationship to the existing campus, specifically a bordering brick Victorian house.

Iconic architecture isn't always an extravagance in material terms. When assessing the cost of a building, it's important to look closely at what is being bought. The Sydney Opera House, designed by Jørn Utzon, came with what seemed to be an appalling cost over the sixteen years of its construction, and the financial overruns were implicated in local protest and political scandal. But it was worth the price. Aside from the instant recognition it brought for the city and the perfect match between structure and setting, there was another key element. When the opera house went into construction

Geodesic dome: A low ratio of structural material to the volume enclosed. Form is a consquence of its technology.

Toronto's Royal Ontario Museum: An extremely high ratio of structural material to volume enclosed. A technology with no relationship to form and no economy of means.

in 1957, the Australian building industry wasn't capable of creating something as sophisticated as Utzon's complex structure. What the opera house paid for was the retooling of the national construction industry. There were lasting benefits and economies that came with its high cost.

It is also helpful to have a recognized standard measure for conservation initiatives. The Leadership in Energy and Environmental Design (LEED) program provides a framework for assessing sustainability and energy efficiency. An American initiative, it was created to define what a "green" building is and it has been adopted internationally. The program helps to check the vagueness of "green," a concept that can imply a number of things and can also be used merely as a marketing term, with little to back it up. What we need now is to translate this program into tax incentives and reduced insurance premiums and to provide immediate rewards, as well as long-term conservation benefits.

Conservation can come in the form of cutting-edge technologies, but it can also be found in ancient principles, some of which have been discarded unnecessarily. As Winston Churchill noted in another context: "If we open a quarrel between the past and the present, we shall find that we have lost the future."

REGENT PARK COMMUNITY HEALTH CENTRE, TORONTO, ONTARIO

The Regent Park Community Health Centre provides clinical health care, counselling and health promotion to the community surrounding Canada's oldest and largest public-housing project. The centre serves a diverse population of approximately 26,000 people, including those living in subsidized housing, as well as some who are either underhoused or homeless. It uses an integrated approach to health care, with a wide range of health and social services that address the complex needs and challenges of area residents. In order to address the broad range of concerns identified by users, the detailed requirements for each room were discussed in the centre with these potential clients. The location of each space within the facility was determined by analyzing the functional relationships between the various areas. This award-winning project has become a source of pride to residents who are not accustomed to high-end services and design.

This central atrium is the means of orientation and a source of light to the interior of the building. There is little need for signage – public reception areas, private clinical areas and service areas are understood by the economy of spatial means to convey messages of place and procedure.

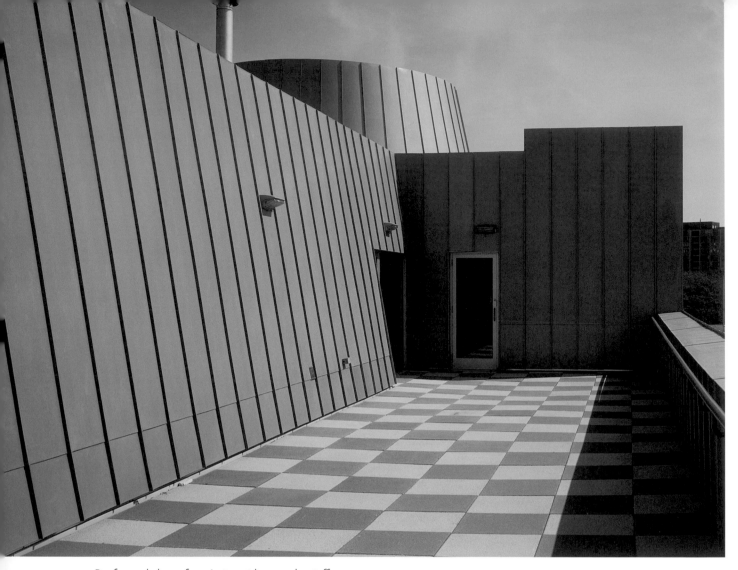

Roofscape balcony for private outdoor use by staff.

The staircase penetrating the atrium makes clear the public access to clinics on upper floors.

Walking track, wood-decked gymnasium and view to heritage woodlot to the left.

CAWTHRA COMMUNITY CENTRE, MISSISSAUGA, ONTARIO

The Cawthra Community Centre is a 3,000-square-metre addition to an existing twin-pad arena. It contains a gymnasium, an active-living studio, multipurpose rooms, a kitchen, teen activity room and newly refurbished arena change rooms. The project is located at the southern edge of the largest stand of native deciduous trees in Mississauga, and the north wall of the gymnasium is completely glazed to provide views of the woodlot, to remove the barrier between inside and outside and protect the exposed south flank of the heritage woods.

Construction systems were selected for their economy of means and efforts were made to reveal the essential nature of the materials used. Finishes are sparse and the colour scheme is largely the by-product of the materials themselves. Timber was selected for its narrative association with the adjacent woodlot and its warm appearance. Reinforced concrete is used in bold cantilevers for the walking track and the second-floor connection to the arenas. Ashlar block in a stack-bond arrangement provides functional utility and reinforces the visual order of horizontal elements. Clear anodized aluminum provides brightness and green-tinted glass reduces solar heat gain and evokes the outside foliage.

Entry lobby.

Orange molded brick evokes the handmade quality of masonry used for some of the region's industrial buildings. Solid brick lintels, in lieu of steel shelf angles, is a rarely used detail that gives crispness and clarity to door and window openings and demonstrates the superior abilities of the project's masons.

MEMORIAL POOL, TORONTO, ONTARIO

As part of a public facility that includes an arena and a public elementary school, the community aquatics centre shares a range of resources with the other buildings in the complex. The centre sits on the edge of Mimico Creek, overlooking the heavily treed areas at the base of its ravine. The natural topography of the site influenced the shape of the facility, which appears as a series of volumes that follow the slope of the land. An existing pedestrian walkway into the ravine has been extended to form a public concourse that runs alongside the pool and ties together the three parts of the community facility.

The centre makes use of its sloping site in a series of terraced areas. Once inside, visitors get their first view of the pool from an upper concourse. In addition to the pool, a health club is situated on the lower level. It is screened from pedestrian traffic by a garden wall that is cut into the earth surrounding the club. Nestled between this wall and the windows of the health club is a terraced garden. The interior finishes include high-grade metals and mahogany.

Project model.

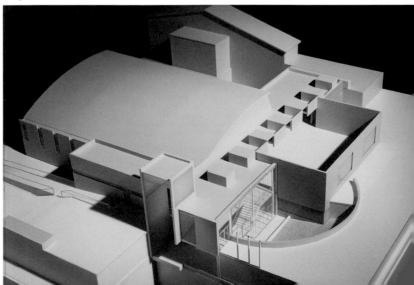

DAVENPORT WING, LASH MILLER CHEMISTRY BUILDING, UNIVERSITY OF TORONTO, TORONTO, ONTARIO

In response to the major transformations in chemistry since the Lash Miller Chemistry Building opened in 1963, a two-storey addition of research laboratories was created. The new wing is dedicated almost exclusively to leading-edge chemical synthesis and research in biological and medicinal chemistry for students in both undergraduate and graduate studies. The new space includes nineteen preparative chemistry laboratories, 121 research-grade fume hoods, eighteen faculty and research offices, service rooms, common rooms, computer laboratories and work areas for theoretical chemistry. The research spaces are characterized by generous windows, light and views, warm wood materials, with carrels for research assistants integrated into the laboratories.

A key objective of the design was to facilitate contact among colleagues. A two-storey interior skylit courtyard was created at the junction of the new wing and the existing research towers. There's a large seminar room nearby, and the new departmental library overlooks the court. The ground-floor lobby has been expanded to merge visually with a re-landscaped campus courtyard. Within the lobby are a juice bar, seating for fifty students and windows that look into teaching laboratories.

A new research wing, constructed of lightweight steel and clad in copper and curtain wall, sits above an existing two-storey brick pavilion of brick masonry.

THAYER BUILDING, UNIVERSITY OF MICHIGAN, ANN ARBOR, MICHIGAN

The new six-storey building is the home of two departments and two institutes that form part of the larger Literature, Science and the Arts Faculty at the University of Michigan.

Designed for an extremely small corner site constrained by existing buildings on its south and west perimeters, this building's plan relies on a tight interior court to accommodate circulation and orientation. A floor at the third level of the court creates a two-storey ground-floor lobby overlooked by library gallery seminar and office spaces. A four-storey upper court brings natural light to the myriad offices and meeting spaces on the upper floors. The interior court provides both informal lounges and study spaces at every level. Constructed with a budget 30 per cent less than conventional academic buildings, the design relies on a simple plan and materials to achieve this objective.

Not by Bread Alone: Building for the Arts

When cultural buildings don't engage their environment, when they exclude the locals – by taste or design or ticket price – they become fortresses.

"I wouldn't mind seeing opera die," Frank Lloyd Wright once said. "Ever since I was a boy, I've regarded opera as a ponderous anachronism." In his lifetime, uncharitable colleagues accused Wright himself of being a ponderous anachronism. Yet opera and Wright's work have both endured, despite occasional assaults and leaky roofs. The death of opera would leave a gaping musical lacuna and deliver a considerable economic impact. Toronto's cultural industries generate almost $2 billion annually in revenue. In New York, London and Paris, the figure is much higher. Cultural activity is an important source of economic growth. It is also one of the most important factors in assessing quality of life, which is as critical to a city's success as location, communications, governance and tax structure.

Early European opera houses were often elevated somewhat and built more grandly than their surroundings, though they were still identifiably part of the urban fabric. Late twentieth-century opera houses and concert halls, in contrast, have tended to be iconic buildings that stand apart from their immediate area. They are frequently the result of architectural competitions, where the goal, stated or unstated, is to find a signature building or at the very least a signature architect.

One of the most infamous competitions was a "blind" competition in 1983 for the Bastille Opera in Paris. The competition's jury didn't know which design was attached to which architect. The story persists that the judges selected an entry they believed had been submitted by Richard Meier. After the winning entry was announced, it turned out that the architect wasn't the famous designer of the High Museum of Art in Atlanta, Georgia, but a young unknown Canadian named Carlos Ott. There was a public outcry, even a sense of betrayal, and the Bastille Opera House became the most controversial of the many *grands travaux* initiated by President François Mitterrand, simply because it challenged the idea of what makes an iconic design. Could the opera house still be a signature building if its signature belonged to an unknown architect?

If a concert hall is designed from the outside in, the acousticians can be left to solve the problem of the sound. Working from the sound out, however, a concert hall expresses its central purpose. DSAI's Four Seasons Centre for the Performing Arts in Toronto was designed both from the outside in, taking its context into account, and from the inside out – a collaboration between the architects, acoustician, theatre planner, and the client, the Canadian Opera Company. It was shaped by sightline and acoustical studies. It isn't only the acoustics that affect a performance and how it is experienced by an audience. The configuration of the interior also plays a role. A curved space brings the audience into closer proximity both to the performers and to itself. People watch and respond as a collective.

All aspects of the design were measured by their service to the goal of an intimate but shared experience of performance and an enhancement of the public life of the city. The Four Seasons Centre represents the resolution of two opposing forces – the centrifugal and the centripetal.

Once the design of the performance area has been conceived, there is the challenge of communicating the building's essence. How does it address the street? The great nineteenth-century opera houses such as Charles Garnier's Paris Opera are magnificent, but they have a formality that reflects the class structure of the time. Opera was an elitist art that was reserved for the wealthy, and typically patrons ascended to a grand entrance. However, in recent decades, opera has been reinvigorated by innovative staging, youthful directors, unconventional interpretations and new works. In Toronto, opera audiences have become more diverse, and it is no longer unusual to see people in their early twenties and thirties at performances. The Four Seasons Centre reflects the evolution of the art and the subsequent democratization of the genre. In contrast to Beaux-Arts planning, where the patron would be greeted by sculpted stone and stairs up to the *piano nobile*, the entrance is at grade level and exterior walls are colourless low-iron glass, giving the building a transparency and a sense of accessibility. "Opera begins long before the curtain goes up," Maria Callas said, "and ends long after it has gone down." The same can be said of opera houses. Their effect, economically, architecturally and culturally, reverberates throughout the life of a city.

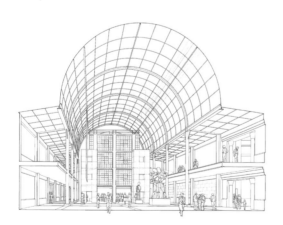 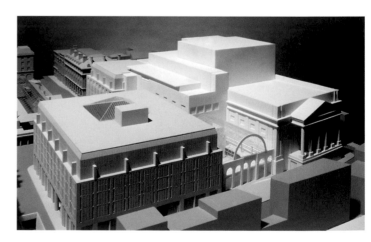

Royal Opera House, Covent Garden competition: This proposal involved both a technically sophisticated and a historically sensitive enlargement and modernization of the Royal Opera House. Work on the theatre complex involved the enlargement of the front-of-house facilities; a new stage, with expanded side and rear stages, and new fly tower, and scenery handling storage, and increased backstage and staff facilities, including three rehearsal halls, dressing rooms, wardrobe storage, green room and offices. The Floral Hall connected to a crush space, green room and entrance from the Covent Garden square.

254

Cultural institutions can also be a force for urban renewal. In 1999, Diamond and Schmitt Architects were retained to renovate and expand the Detroit Symphony's Orchestra Hall. This historic concert hall was plagued with a serious deficit and a challenging location, though the 1919 structure still possessed some of the best acoustics for symphonic music in the country. The decision to renovate and expand Orchestra Hall prompted a campaign to raise $125 million, most of which came from private donors. It became a de facto urban renewal project.

In order to affect the surrounding area, the designers of the new building had to recognize its problems and embrace what was most vital. Detroit had a respected orchestra, but as the birthplace of Motown the city has historically been known for other musical genres – notably R&B, hip hop, rap and jazz. In renovating this facility, these musical traditions were incorporated into the new structure. The 2,000-seat venue retains its marvellous acoustical properties, but the addition of two smaller halls, seating 500 and 175 patrons, allows for other kinds of shows. So, while the Detroit Symphony plays Mahler in the main hall, hip hop and jazz can be heard in the building's neighbouring concert spaces.

The Detroit Symphony's Orchestra Hall was conceived as a common ground for the city's musical genres and their different constituencies, a way to bridge a racial divide. The building itself engages the street and has reconnected itself to the city. Orchestra Hall has become the focal point for a music centre that includes an new recital hall and the Detroit High School for the Fine Performing and Communication Arts. There is an educational program within Orchestra Hall where symphony members teach master classes, as well as an outreach program that involves the high school. Music is an intrinsic and inclusive expression of Detroit's character, and the building was designed to reflect and promote that spirit.

When cultural buildings – whether opera houses or hockey arenas – don't engage their immediate environment, or when they exclude local residents by taste or design or the price of tickets, they can become fortresses. As such, whatever their perceived aesthetic merits, they have failed at a critical level. There is an urgent need for cultural institutions to foster community.

FOUR SEASONS CENTRE FOR THE PERFORMING ARTS, TORONTO, ONTARIO
The Four Seasons Centre for the Performing Arts, opened in 2006, occupies an entire block at one of Toronto's busiest intersections, Queen Street and University Avenue.

Richard Bradshaw Amphitheatre

CANADIAN OPERA COMPANY CAPITAL CAMPAIGN · FOUR SEASONS CENTRE

The Richard Bradshaw Amphitheatre, visible from University Avenue, is the location for more than 100 free concerts annually. This multipurpose space allows the Canadian Opera Company to fulfill its mandate to create an inviting, animated and engaging opera house.

The horseshoe-shaped auditorium gives the audience a sense of itself and creates a close relationship between performer and patron.

Comprised of five key components, including the auditorium and stages, lobby, orchestra pit and back-of-house areas, the new structure provides a permanent home for the Canadian Opera Company and the National Ballet of Canada.

Built acoustically for the needs of opera, the 2,000-seat auditorium is a building within a building: Its heavy double structure and rubber isolation pads make it impenetrable to all unwanted sound and vibration. The traditional European horseshoe design has five levels of shallow balconies and unobstructed sightlines. The auditorium is only 28 metres wide, with the first row of the balconies only 27 metres from the stage. Thus, almost 75 per cent of the seats are within 30 metres of centre stage.

Light, transparency and delicacy are in dramatic contrast to the opacity and monolithic enclosure of the auditorium and stage. Passing from one space to another is to move from a heightened sense of the city to the intimate experience of music, drama and dance.

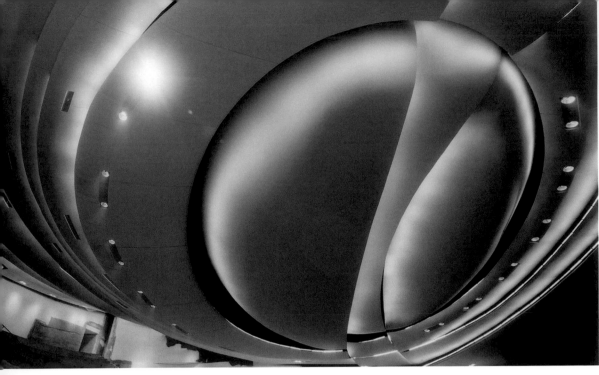

The curves of the ceiling conceal both a control booth and lighting positions and provide the apertures for return air. While delicate in appearance, they are made of 5-centimetre-thick plaster designed to reflect sound to every corner of the auditorium.

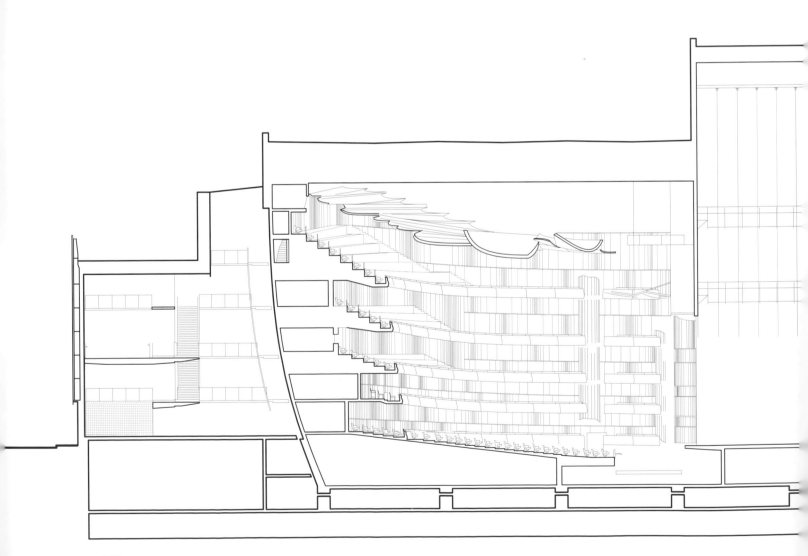

The glass stairs give lightness and transparency to both the space
and the movement within the space.

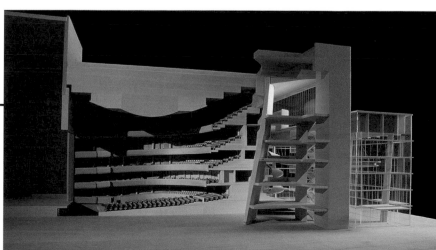

This lantern of light in the city also illuminates the activities within and frames views for patrons of the surrounding city. The excitement and anticipation of performances is enhanced for the audience and the passerby equally.

GARTER LANE ARTS CENTRE, WATERFORD, IRELAND

Garter Lane Arts Centre is home to a vibrant and extensive program that includes dance, theatre, film, live music and fine arts. Productions range from contemporary Irish to international, professional and amateur productions. The centre is located in a 1790 Quaker meeting house in downtown Waterford, on the southeast coast of Ireland.

Diamond and Schmitt Architects led the design of the much-needed renovations and additions to the theatre, providing new washrooms, kitchen, dressing rooms, box office, administrative offices and backstage facilities.

The 215-seat auditorium and stage have been reconfigured to improve sightlines and crossover space behind the stage. The new work was combined with restoration of this historically significant site.

MAX M. FISHER MUSIC CENTER, DETROIT, MICHIGAN

Constructed in six months in 1919, the 2,000-seat Symphony Hall, listed on the National Register of Historic Places, has accoustics that are among the very best in North America. Nevertheless, it was abandoned and derelict until the musicians led its initial restoration in the early 1990s. Diamond and Schmitt completed the restoration, installing state-of-the-art heating, ventilation and air-conditioning services.

The restoration of the 4,650-square-metre hall was combined with the addition of 12,000 square metres, including new Concert Hall, a Rehearsal Hall accessible for small public performances, and the best suites of musician support space available in the nation.

A Music Education Center supports eleven youth ensembles and the youth orchestra. At the heart of the centre, a new four-storey lobby court, glamorous with Venetian plaster and bronze detail, provides connection and gathering spaces for the revitalized and new audiences for the broad range of music now performed in the centre.

The Symphony Hall (1919) has been restored with state-of-the-art mechanical and electrical services to support the highest performance standard.

A new lobby provides flexible audience space and serves as a crossroads between the Symphony Hall, Music Box and the Rehearsal Hall. A large window, whose scale and five-bay proportion match the inset stone facade of this heritage symphony hall, makes the energetic programs of the centre visible to the community.

The lobby's palette of bronze sapele wood, glass lanterns and steel create a glamorous environment, which emulates, in wooden detail, the traditions of historic Detroit theatres.

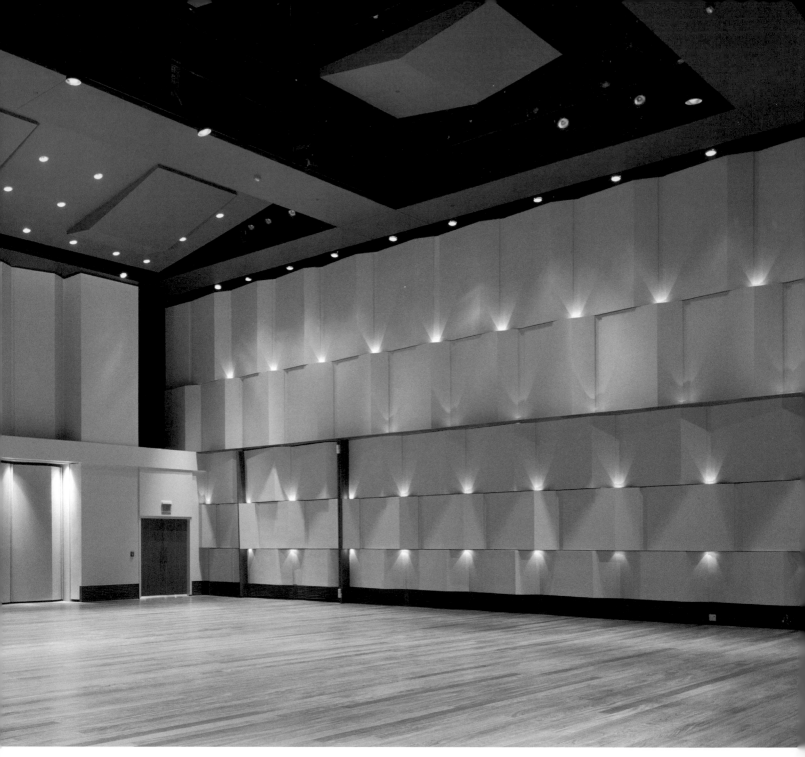

The flexible Music Box transforms from a flat-floor reception and
performance space to a raked theatre that seats 450 people.

Generous connections between performance space and lobby allow different audiences to interact.

AGNES ETHERINGTON ART CENTRE, QUEEN'S UNIVERSITY
KINGSTON, ONTARIO

Designed to house the university's major art collections, including the Bader Collection of seventeenth- and eighteenth-century European art, the Agnes Etherington Art Centre is a lively gathering place for scholars, artists, students and the public. The complex is a joint partnership between the City of Kingston and Queen's University, serving as both art gallery and art-conservation facility.

The complex includes a large art studio for classes and school programs, a multipurpose hall for lectures and receptions, a retail outlet, an art rental program, storage vaults and support facilities. This integrated mix gives the centre significant flexibility as a public venue. The project includes 930 square metres of gallery space, a 930-square-metre vault, and a further 1,070 square metres of multipurpose room and support space. The building, which houses two Rembrandts, meets the highest standards for temperature, humidity and lighting control.

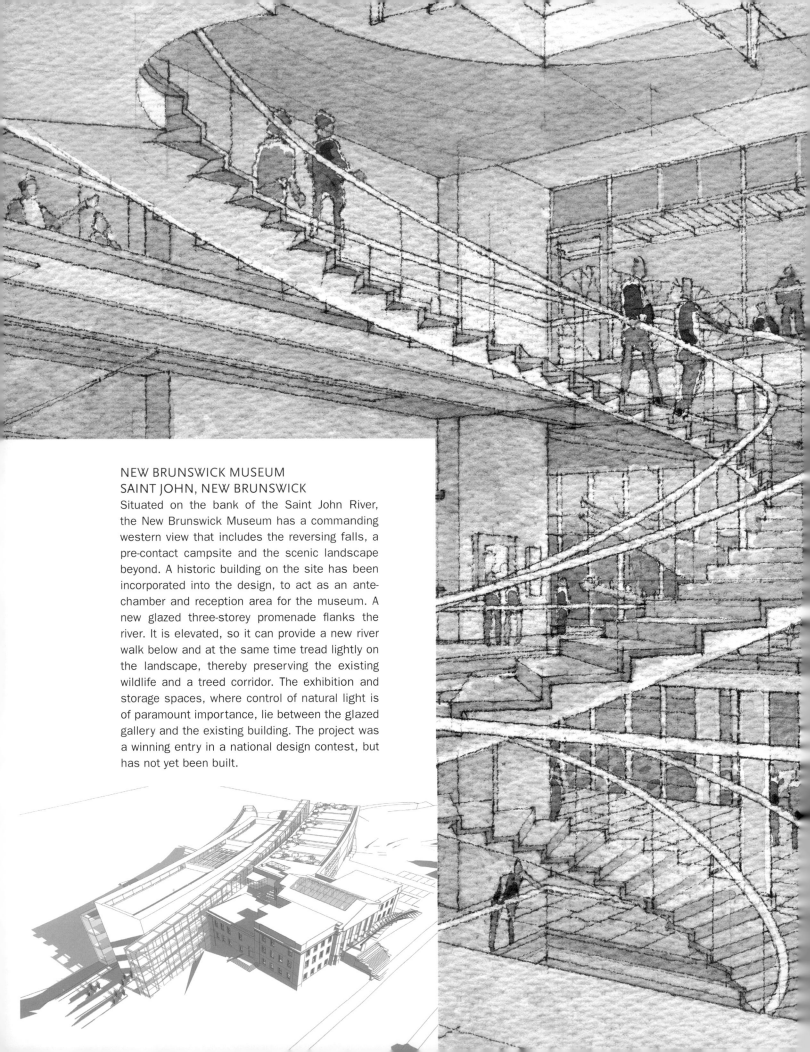

NEW BRUNSWICK MUSEUM
SAINT JOHN, NEW BRUNSWICK

Situated on the bank of the Saint John River, the New Brunswick Museum has a commanding western view that includes the reversing falls, a pre-contact campsite and the scenic landscape beyond. A historic building on the site has been incorporated into the design, to act as an ante-chamber and reception area for the museum. A new glazed three-storey promenade flanks the river. It is elevated, so it can provide a new river walk below and at the same time tread lightly on the landscape, thereby preserving the existing wildlife and a treed corridor. The exhibition and storage spaces, where control of natural light is of paramount importance, lie between the glazed gallery and the existing building. The project was a winning entry in a national design contest, but has not yet been built.

COUNTRY DAY SCHOOL, PERFORMING ARTS CENTRE, KING CITY, ONTARIO

The Performing Arts Centre contains a 350-seat flexible theatre designed for the drama and music departments of this private school. In addition to the theatre, the centre includes a rehearsal hall, music and drama classrooms, a mid-sized laboratory and practice rooms. The centre also contains a workshop, stage pit, wardrobe maintenance classroom and two twelve-person dressing rooms. The 3,000-square-metre theatre has a floor that can be changed to a theatre-in-the-round, proscenium or flat-floor configuration. The seating is a combination of raked retractable and fixed forms.

The main performance space has two lighting gallery levels, catwalks, a balcony level and a control room. A second control room is located adjacent to one of the English and drama classrooms, which can also be used for small performances and as rehearsal space. The simple design enables school children to operate all aspects of the stage and auditorium. The Performing Arts Centre's colonnade and timber entrance resembles a marquee, large enough for a gathering area before and after performances. In addition, the facility includes two side courtyards: a side colonnade opening towards the east and a glazed colonnade enclosing an existing courtyard to the north.

A Lesson in Building: Spaces for Education

While disciplines are converging, university buildings are becoming more separated and isolated.

When Thomas Jefferson, architect, inventor and the third president of the United States, imagined a campus for the University of Virginia in 1817, he wanted to dovetail educational and aesthetic goals. He believed that the quality of the environment would determine the quality of the education. Jefferson's campus, which he described as an "Academical Village," was self-sufficient, set apart from the city of Charlottesville, and it featured a central green space as its organizing principle – much like a town square.

The Jeffersonian ideal became a model for many North American campuses. As these campuses, including the original, expanded, however, they often lost the initial clarity and scale that made them so effective and appealing. The growth of university campuses mimics the growth of many cities: an unorganized sprawl where the aesthetic fabric, pathways and defined exterior spaces begin to fray, causing the community to become physically fractured.

The architectural evolution of many North American campuses follows a recognizable pattern. There are the original heritage buildings, usually some unambitious institutional structures, a few modernist structures and postmodern buildings that include a few historical references. Over the years, campus architecture has become increasingly diverse, and there is often a tenuous relationship between the buildings. As satellite campuses are built in distant suburbs, the university itself is being balkanized.

At the same time, the boundaries between academic disciplines are dissolving at universities everywhere. Life science faculties engage engineers, planners, economists and philosophers within them. Medical research involves the contribution and scrutiny of ethicists, lawyers, venture capitalists and information technology and robotics engineers. Because university faculties are being redefined, academic buildings for teaching and research need to facilitate increased interdisciplinary interaction, while still maintaining departmental and disciplinary delineation. One of the challenges in designing university buildings is reconciling these two contrary trends: buildings that are becoming more separate and isolated, and disciplines that are converging. What is needed is an architecture that encourages dialogue between people and disciplines.

In creating spaces for a university, the nature of education itself is sometimes overlooked. Today, most buildings are constructed amid financial pressures to realize as much functional space as possible, and to reduce the ratio between a building's square footage and its usable area. But in designing university buildings, this demand can be a false economy, one that doesn't view education and research in the wider sense. Formal knowledge is transmitted in lecture halls, but new knowledge is often the result of casual interaction. Many developments and breakthroughs have resulted from chance meetings between individuals in informal environments, and architecture can foster such environments. Older university buildings often have generous stairways and landings, places that easily become de facto rooms and sites for unplanned encounters. Hallways that are wide enough to congregate in, eating and lounging areas that are well situated, and atriums that bring light to the centre of a building and promote connectivity between floors are all ways to encourage interaction.

The formal teaching spaces are equally critical. Lecture halls, especially large lecture halls, can be built on the same principles that govern the design of a concert hall or theatre. Like any audience, students benefit from good sightlines and acoustics. And the configuration of the room can change the dynamic of the class. If the students are facing the lecturer from tiered rows that rise in parallel lines away from the front of the room, they tend to listen as individuals. In an elliptical room, they are inclined towards one another, as well, and the shape promotes a collective experience.

The research component of universities is also evolving. In the 1960s and 1970s, the prevailing ethic for designing research facilities favoured windowless laboratories. The need for seclusion, and sometimes secrecy, was interpreted architecturally as a bunker, and this attitude became accepted wisdom. But the nature of research has changed in three decades, and there is now a greater need for interaction between both colleagues and disciplines. It is possible to facilitate collaboration without compromising privacy, and to bring natural light to laboratories.

An intimate 250-seat elliptical lecture theatre at the University of Ontario Institute of Technology.

University of Ontario Institute of Technology: Colonnades provide weather-protected connection between academic disciplines.

The role of the university itself is changing as the knowledge-based economy grows, we manufacture less and we divert more resources to research and the compilation and analysis of data. The concept of the ivory tower is disappearing under a network of corporate alliances with a variety of university departments, practical applications for academic research and the use of new technologies everywhere. The work that goes on at universities is now a catalyst for the regeneration of cities. The barriers that traditionally existed between the campus and the city have eroded, as universities have become less elitist, more secular and more integrated into the economy.

As the role of universities changes and they become more competitive, vying for talent, students and money, they often behave like the private sector. In this entrepreneurial environment, iconic architecture is sometimes used as a means to draw attention to the campus. The drawback to this approach is not just its lack of context, it also presents a pragmatic issue. The evolving nature of technology and the way disciplines interconnect means that buildings must have some built-in flexibility. The ability to reconfigure the space, to have some leeway in the delivery of electricity, data, ventilation and heat is important. The indulgence of the architect can easily limit the scope of the building's future uses.

The word campus is Latin for "field," and as Jefferson noted, the land is a critical element of the educational experience. Yet university landscapes are sometimes little more than the residual space left over after the siting of built structures. The landscape and the spaces between buildings should have an important function. They can be shaped to define outdoor rooms and places of expansive or intimate scale, and they become the connective tissue that links disparate structures into a coherent and legible whole. A walk through any campus demonstrates how and where students tend to congregate. Well-calibrated landscapes and urban elements, whether in the form of colonnades that connect buildings, quadrangles that organize them, or courtyards that provide some respite from the crowd, are critical to building a collegial community.

Architectural evolution is sometimes nothing more than the blind following of a trend. What appears to be progress is actually inertia. It is healthy and necessary to challenge assumptions; to search for new materials, technologies, forms and economies that best express a building's purpose; and to create spaces – both interior and exterior – that awe us not with pyrotechnics but with the elegance of ideas. Universities are rooted in tradition, yet charged with the role of innovation. It is important to recognize this inherent tension, to understand education in its changing nature, and to accommodate its potential.

A classroom in the Computer Science and Engineering Building at the University of Michigan.

are the total assets in each city? Order alphabetically by city.

select bcity as City, sum(assets) as "Total Assets"
from branch
group by bcity
order by bcity;

City	Total Assets
Bennington	300000
Brooklyn	16100000
⋮	

ACADEMIC LIBRARY, UNIVERSITY OF ONTARIO INSTITUTE OF TECHNOLOGY, OSHAWA, ONTARIO

With its 650 fully computer-connected workspaces and electronic classrooms, as well as its dramatic, three-storey glass rotunda, the library at the University of Ontario Institute of Technology in Oshawa, Ontario, is a showplace for the twenty-first century.

Much attention has been paid to the quality and variety of student space in this facility. Large study halls overlook the landscaped commons and provide a variety of table, carrel and lounge seating. Enclosed rooms are provided for group study, seminar discussion and quiet work activities. A small sixty-seat café in the library overlooks a reflecting pool/ice rink and a stormwater management pond. The library houses a print collection of about 125,000 books, with a significant emphasis on reference material, but it is the provision of wired and wireless connection to electronic collections that distinguishes it from libraries in most other post-secondary institutions.

Main study hall.

View of the library from the stormwater management pond.

Exterior sun-shading reduces solar gain while still allowing abundant natural light in study areas.

East facade.

Study carrels.

A quiet reading room with fireplace.

COMPUTER SCIENCE AND ENGINEERING BUILDING, UNIVERSITY OF MICHIGAN, ANN ARBOR, MICHIGAN

The Computer Science and Engineering Building houses teaching and research space for faculty and graduate students. With its complex research including robotics and artificial intelligence, it is one of the premier computer science schools in the United States.

The different laboratory groups, faculty and students had previously been housed in various locations on the campus, and they are now consolidated in one building specifically designed to meet their needs. The interior space is open, filled with natural light and fosters an atmosphere of interaction and vibrancy. The building contains a skylit gathering place – an open interior court with a staircase, which follows the slope of the hilly site and connects all floors.

The site both fronts onto the North Campus Commons, designed by Eero Saarinen, and forms a bridge up a steeply rising topography to the north. A continuous outdoor stair and ramp allows students to access the site through new landscaped courtyards to the residences at the north.

A skylit stair steps down four storeys and connects
students and faculty throughout the building.

Detail of the exterior facade.

A fragment of the ENIAC (Electronic Numerical Integrator and Computer), the first large-scale general-purpose electronic computer developed in part by faculty at the University of Michigan, is displayed in the entry vestibule.

The dramatic circular stair, located in the atrium, links all floors of the building and facilitates interaction and chance encounters between faculty and students as they move throughout the space.

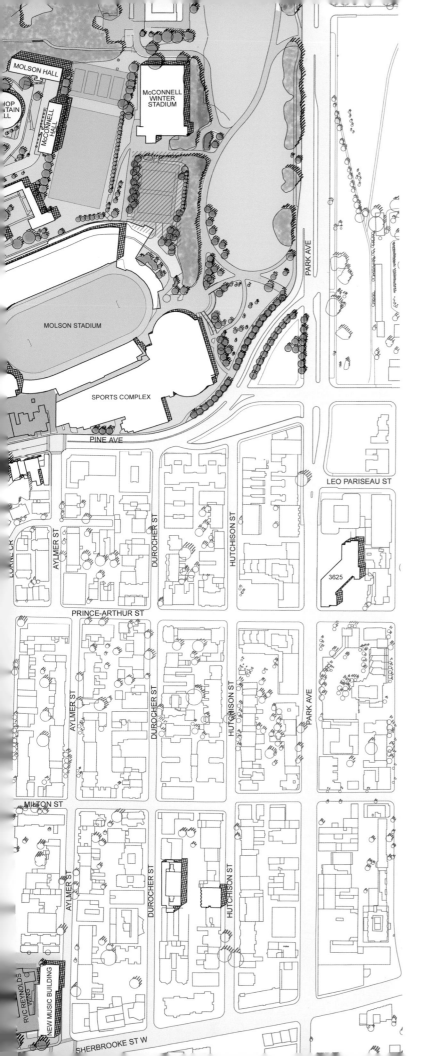

MOLSON HALL

McCONNELL
WINTER
STADIUM

McCONNELL HALL

MOLSON STADIUM

SPORTS COMPLEX

PINE AVE

PARK AVE

LEO PARISEAU ST

AYLMER ST

DUROCHER ST

HUTCHISON ST

3625

PRINCE-ARTHUR ST

AYLMER ST

DUROCHER ST

HUTCHISON ST

PARK AVE

MILTON ST

AYLMER ST

DUROCHER ST

HUTCHISON ST

RVC REYNOLDS WING

NEW MUSIC BUILDING

SHERBROOKE ST W

CAMPUS MASTER PLAN, MCGILL UNIVERSITY, MONTREAL, QUEBEC

Diamond and Schmitt were retained in 2005 by McGill University to undertake a multi-campus master plan to guide the institution's physical development for the next twenty to twenty-five years. The physical layout extends from Mount Royal Park to the north and the city of Montreal to the south, east and west. This physical master plan is driven by a new academic goal: to provide the vehicle for the university to achieve a "top 10" ranking among the world's research institutions. The McGill project also addresses governance, to ensure that this goal can be implemented.

The master plan provides a comprehensive vision for the development of the McGill campuses, including the grounds, facilities and infrastructure. It is broad and flexible in outlook and able to accommodate changing needs, opportunities and priorities over an extended period. Future developments will be directed in such a manner that every project contributes to the quality and coherence of the university as a whole, while still satisfying the needs of the users of each facility.

The plan makes a distinction between the permanent armature of the streets, public spaces and the building site. Via the provision of building standards, the plan allows for permanence and provides the ability to make changes when needed.

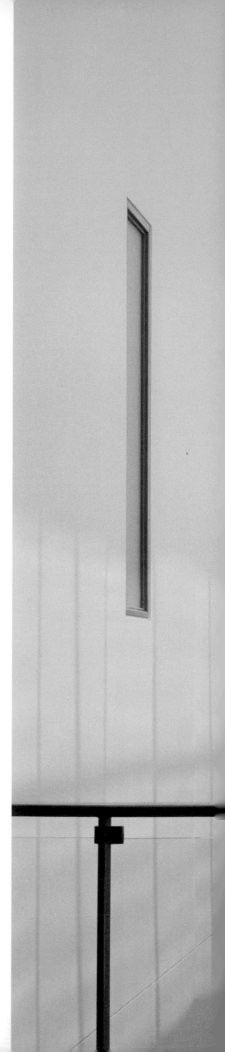

ANTHONY P. TOLDO HEALTH EDUCATION CENTRE, UNIVERSITY OF WINDSOR, WINDSOR, ONTARIO

The Health Education Centre is an 7,900-square-metre teaching building accommodating 1,000 students. The new centre is equipped with state-of-the-art learning technologies in classrooms, providing flexible teaching and learning environments in a variety of classrooms up to 285 seats in size. The building also houses faculty offices for the School of Nursing and is adjacent to the new Medical School.

Much effort has been invested in the design of student gathering places, a café, and nooks for informal study and discussion. These spaces are designed to foster a collegial environment that complements the more formal teaching environments provided within classroom and seminar spaces.

302

SCHOOL OF IMAGE ARTS, RYERSON UNIVERSITY, TORONTO, ONTARIO

The School of Image Arts at Ryerson University is a teaching and research facility in the areas of photography, film and new media. The university recently acquired the Black Star Collection of twentieth-century photojournalism. With more than 300,000 images by the century's leading photographers, the collection suddenly catapulted the university into the position of a leading institution in the presentation, preservation and collecting of photographic history.

The project has two program components. A 1,860-square-metre gallery and graduate research centre are accommodated within the existing three-storey brick structure (a former brewery), and a new two-storey entry loggia to the centre, constructed on a former lane adjacent to landscaped open space, provides visibility and presence for the gallery, as well as study space. A new four-storey addition built above the roof of the existing building contains academic studio, teaching and faculty space. It takes advantage of the existing property lines to extend a transparent sheath over the existing building, bringing stairs, student lounges and study spaces down to ground level and animating all seven storeys with vibrant activity.

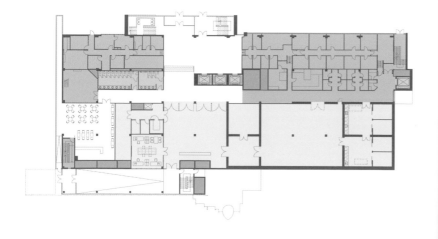

EARTH SCIENCES CENTRE, UNIVERSITY OF TORONTO, TORONTO, ONTARIO

The Earth Sciences Centre is a 30,000-square-metre teaching and research complex, which provides a cross-disciplinary home for the Departments of Botany and Geology, and the Faculty of Forestry at the University of Toronto.

Included in the building program are more than 10,000 square metres of technologically advanced research laboratories, a 400-seat auditorium, lecture halls, student facilities, and common areas. These are designed to encourage interaction among students, faculty, and the different academic disciplines. At the heart of the complex, a 125,000-volume library integrates combined disciplines.

The project broke new ground in the design of research and teaching facilities. Laboratories are built to modular dimensions and are serviced to allow easy changes to benching and equipment. Fume hoods were modified to act as a return air system, achieving a greater degree of personal safety than normal and saving the cost of a ducted return air system. In contrast to most lab facilities of the previous two decades, each lab and office has large windows for natural light.

The design reactivated the surrounding urban area and reunited it with the campus. Quadrangles, courtyards and colonnades, together with building forms clad in brick and stone, were some of the devices used to achieve this goal.

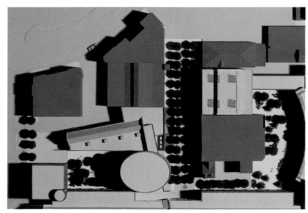

SCHOOL OF COMPUTER SCIENCE AND ENGINEERING,
THE HEBREW UNIVERSITY OF JERUSALEM, JERUSALEM, ISRAEL

A state-of-the-art graduate teaching facility, the School of Engineering and Computer Science is designed to accommodate a department of 1,250 students. Housing a variety of laboratories, an auditorium and seminar and office spaces, the school is the pre-eminent institution of its kind in Israel and a world leader in software design and computer technology.

The centrepiece of the project is the Albert Einstein Archives, an independent pavilion designed to exhibit and store artifacts that once belonged to the influential scientist. As well, the school contains more than 1,115 square metres of laboratory space devoted to advanced materials research and nanotechnology, with Class 100 clean-room facilities. The building completes the edge of a prominent pedestrian promenade while addressing stringent urban design principles such as height limitation, conformity with the landscape and the retention of views.

BAHEN CENTRE FOR INFORMATION TECHNOLOGY, UNIVERSITY OF TORONTO, TORONTO, ONTARIO
The Bahen Centre for Information Technology is designed to facilitate cross-disciplinary teaching and research for both the Faculty of Arts and Science and the Faculty of Engineering at the University of Toronto. The building, based on the concept of a high-tech loft space, is designed to achieve an outstanding level of flexibility in program, configuration, and servicing.

A skylit arcade provides pedestrian connections throughout the building. A circular stair stands at the crossroads of the plan, surrounding a tower of shared meeting rooms and linking all eight levels. The glass cylinder is skylit, drawing daylight deep into the building. A two-storey interior court overlooks the landscaped quadrangle, which is enclosed by existing buildings. The driveway between the adjacent Fields Institute and the Koffler Centre for Student Services has been transformed into a pedestrian walk, lined with trees and bordered by a rivulet of water flowing from the quadrangle pool. A circular tower that houses faculty offices and meeting areas takes advantage of the low height of adjacent buildings to provide natural light and views. Along St. George Street the building steps down to three storeys in height to match the cornice of the Koffler Centre. This wing envelopes a designated historic Victorian house in a small courtyard opening off the street. A pavilion emulating the proportions of the house was extended to the north, its translucent glass link forming a backdrop to the Victorian building. The pavilion on the corner helps to establish the Bahen Centre's presence at this important intersection within the university.

A tall arcade bisects the urban block, connects to the adjacent heritage Student Centre and provides access to numerous lecture theatres and seminar rooms on the first three storeys.

A circular stair at the crossroads of the north-south and east-west routes through the centre rises eight storeys, to form a vertical public access for encounter and interaction. Top lit by skylight, the glass cladding and fibre optic tracery draw daylight deep into the plan.

An existing Victorian house was retained and restored and frames a minor entry court.

View of central stair and skylight.

Delicate transparency contrasts with robust masonry on the north facade.

A former service driveway was transformed to create a new campus gateway from the city. Stormwater, collected and stored in an arcade of two-storey cisterns within a new midblock quadrangle, irrigates the new landscape and flows in a handrail channel as a welcome gesture of entry.

319

PROJECT LIST

CONSULTANTS
Structural = (S)
Mechanical = (M)
Electrical = (E)
Acoustics = (A)
Theatre Planning = (T)
Cost = (C)
Civil = (Ci)
General Contractor = (GC)
Construction Manager = (GC)
Landscape = (L)
Laboratory = (La)
Urban Planning = (UP)
Heritage = (H)
Museum = (MU)
Joint Venture = (JV)

Agnes Etherington Art Centre, Kingston, Ontario
Client: Queens University

JV Partner: Shoalts and Zaback Architects Ltd.
DSAI Team: Donald Schmitt, Gary McCluskie

Branka Gazibara, Desmond Gregg, Thom Pratt,
Paul Szaszkiewicz

Consultants: Blackwell Bowick Partnership Ltd.
(S), Smith and Anderson Consulting Engineering
(M), Stantec (E)

Alumbrera House, Mustique, The Grenadines
Client: The Lundins

DSAI Team: A.J. Diamond, Dalibor Cizek, Courtenay
Henry

**Anthony P. Toldo Health Education Centre,
Windsor, Ontario**
Client: University of Windsor

Associate Architects: Di Maio Design Associates|
Architect Inc.

DSAI Team: Donald Schmitt, Sydney Browne

Steve Choe, Jayashri Deshmukh, Desmond
Gregg, Sarah Low, Leo Mieles, Don Ryan

Consultants: Halcrow Yolles (S), Crossey
Engineering Ltd. (M, E), ENVision – The Hough
Group (L), Curran McCabe Ravindran Ross
Inc. (C), Aercoustics Engineering Ltd. (A),
Engineering Harmonics Inc. (A), Buttcon Ltd.
(GC)

The Apotex Centre, Toronto, Ontario
Client: Baycrest Centre for Geriatric Care

JV Partner: Boigon Petroff Shepherd Architects
DSAI Team: A.J. Diamond, Gregory Colucci,
Mary Jane Finlayson, George Przybylski

Paul Bakewich, Tania Bortolotto, Desmond
Gregg, Seth Isnar, Birgit Siber, Chris Stevens,
Paul Szaszkiewicz

Consultants: Halcrow Yolles (S), FCE Group
Ltd. (M, E), Vertechs Design inc. (L), PCL
Constructors Canada Ltd. (GC)

**Bahen Centre for Information Technology,
Toronto, Ontario**
Client: University of Toronto

DSAI Team: Donald Schmitt, David Dow,
Michael Leckman, Thom Pratt, Matthew Lella

Stephen Bauer, James Blendick, Constantinos
Catsaros, Terry Cecil, Kirsten Douglas, Ian
Douglas, Natalie Drago, Dan Gallivan,
Desmond Gregg, Michael Gross, Courtenay
Henry, Agnes Kazmierczak, Edward Kim, Dan
Klinck, Frank Mazzulla, Dale McDowell, Leo
Mieles, Dominique Morazain, Sony Rai, Diana
Saragossa, Jon Soules, Jennifer Trost

Consultants: Read Jones Christoffersen
Consulting Engineers Ltd. (S), Stantec (M),
Crossey Engineering Ltd. (E), Ian Gray &
Associates Ltd. (L), Altus Helyar Cost Consulting
(C), PCL Constructors Canada Inc. (GC)

**The Banff Centre – Campus Master Plan and
Implementation, Banff, Alberta**
Client: Banff Centre

Associate Architects: Gibbs Gage Architects
DSAI Team: A.J. Diamond, David Dow, Ana
Maria Llanos, Jarle Lovlin

Mark Cichy, Zvonimir Cicvaric, Leonardo de
Melo, Kent Eliuk, Charles Gagnon, Jim Graves,
Bruce Han, Sarah Low, Carl Madsen, Ryan
Mitchell, Derek Newby, Regina Thian, Michael
Treacy, Jessie Waese, Joe Zingaro

Consultants: Read Jones Christoffersen
Consulting Engineers Ltd. (S), Smith and
Anderson Consulting Engineering Ltd. (M),
Mulvey + Banani International Inc. (E), du Toit
Allsopp Hillier (L), Curran McCabe Ravindran
Ross Inc. (C), PCL Constructors Canada Inc.
(GC)

**Bank Street Building Competition, Ottawa,
Ontario**
Client: Public Works and Government Services
Canada

Associate Architects: KWC Architects

DSAI Team: Donald Schmitt, Martin Davidson,
Dan Klinck

Charles Gagnon, Michael Leckman, Farid Noufaily, Graeme Reed, Malini Rao Smirnis, Erik Sziraki, Florin Tanasoiu, Sybil Wa, Gary Watson

Consultants: Halcrow Yolles (S), Cleland Jardine Alliance Partnership (S), Smith and Andersen Consulting Engineering (M), Mulvey + Banani International Inc. (E), du Toit Allsopp Hillier (L), Martin Conboy Lighting Design (Lighting)

Berkeley Castle, Toronto, Ontario
Client: Berkeley Castle Investments

DSAI Team: A.J. Diamond, George Friedman

Consultants: Halcrow Yolles (S), Hidi Rae Consulting Engineers Inc. (M, E), Vermeulens Cost Consultants (C), Fairway Construction (GC)

Betty Oliphant Theatre, Toronto, Ontario
Client: Canada's National Ballet School

DSAI Team: A.J. Diamond, Donald Schmitt, Victor Jaunkalns

Cheryl Atkinson, John Chandler, Anne-Marie Flemming, Pat Hanson, Charles Hazel, David Miller

Consultants: Halcrow Yolles (S), Bayes, Yates, McMillan Inc. (M), Mulvey + Banani International Inc. (E), Vermeulens Cost Consultants (C), Theatre Projects Consultants Inc. (T), Artec Consultants Inc. (A), Vanbots Construction Corporation (GC)

Cambridge City Hall, Cambridge, Ontario
Client: City of Cambridge

DSAI Team: Donald Schmitt, Gary McCluskie, Branka Gazibara

Robert Boyd, Tai Chi, Aaron Costain, Donna Dolan, Adrian Politano, Diana Saragosa, Michael Waring

Consultants: Read Jones Christoffersen Consulting Engineers Ltd. (S), MCW Consultants Ltd. (M, E), Curran McCabe Ravindran Ross Inc. (C), Fleisher Ridout Partnership Inc. (L), Vanbots Construction Corporation (GC)

Campus Master Plan, Montreal, Quebec
Client: McGill University

JV Partner: du Toit Allsop Hillier
DSAI Team: A.J. Diamond, Sydney Browne Walton Chan, Kirsten Douglas, Robert Graham, Michael Fok, Bruce Han, Andrea Lacalamita, Hilary Pinnington

Canadian Chancery, Prague, Czech Republic
Client: Department of Foreign Affairs

Associate Architects: Aukett Europe
DSAI Team: A.J. Diamond, Jon Soules

Courtenay Henry, Jana Lyskova, Bill Rawlings, Sandor Rott

Consultants: Halcrow Yolles (S), Janecek & Rubasek (S), Smith and Anderson Consulting Engineering (M), Jiri Petlach Vzdvchotechnika (M), Crossey Engineering Ltd. (E), Althelier L (E), Vermeulens Cost Consultants (C), Konstruktiva Konsit (GC)

Capital Information Centre, Ottawa, Ontario
Client: National Capital Commission

DSAI Team: A.J. Diamond, Stewart Adams

Mary Jane Finlayson, George Przybylski, Chris Stevens, Mike Yuen

Consultants: Halsall Engineering Consultants (S), Crossey Engineering Ltd. (M, E), Kees Verburg and Associates (L), Vermeulens Cost Consultants (C), Hanscomb (C), PCL Contractors Eastern Inc. (GC)

Cawthra Community Centre, Mississauga, Ontario
Client: City of Mississauga

DSAI Team: Donald Schmitt, Gregory Colucci Branka Gazibara, Desmond Gregg, Courtenay Henry, Anna Kogan, Gowri Shanker, Mike Yuen

Consultants: Blackwell Bowick Partnership Ltd. (S), Jain & Associates (M, E), Ferris + Associates Inc. (L), Vermeulens Cost Consultants (C), Atlas Corporation (GC)

Centre for Advanced Manufacturing and Design Technologies, Brampton, Ontario
Client: Sheridan College

DSAI Team: Donald Schmitt, Michael Leckman, Charles Gagnon

Francesco Bisci, James Blendick, Aaron Costain, Tony Diodati, Donna Dolan, Kent Eliuk, Desmond Gregg, Theo Kelaiditis, Graeme Reed, Malini Rao Smirnis

Consultants: Read Jones Christoffersen Consulting Engineers Ltd. (S), MCW Consultants Ltd. (M, E), du Toit Allsopp Hillier (L), Bondfield Construction (GC)

Charlie Condominiums, Toronto, Ontario
Client: Great Gulf Group

DSAI Team: Donald Schmitt, David Dow, Steve Bondar

Duncan Bates, Michael Donaldson, Jamie Duncan, Dan Gallivan, Jonathan King, Persis Lam, Breck McFarlane, Doug Richardson, Adam Thom, Gary Watson, Han Xu

Consultants: Read Jones Christoffersen Consulting Engineers Ltd. (S), Able Engineering (M, E), Janet Rosenberg + Associates (L), Tucker Hi-Rise Construction Inc. (GC)

College Residence, Lakeshore Campus, Toronto, Ontario
Client: Humber College

DSAI Team: Donald Schmitt, Mark Berest

Thomas Caro, Elena Chernyshov, Geoffrey Hodgetts, Forde Johnson, Andrew Lind, Don Ryan, Birgit Siber, Caroline Spigelski

Consultants: Read Jones Christoffersen Consulting Engineers Ltd. (S), MCW Consultants Ltd. (M, E), Ferris + Associates Inc. (L), Curran McCabe Ravindran Ross Inc. (C), Eastern Construction (GC), Aercoustics Engineering Ltd. (A), Gamsby and Mannerow Engineers (Ci)

College Residence, North Campus, Toronto, Ontario
Client: Humber College

DSAI Team: Donald Schmitt, Caroline Spigeski

James Blendick, Steve Bondar, Peter Brigden, Michele Gucciardi, Forde Johnson, Michael Lukasik, Don Ryan, Donald Schmitt, Birgit Siber, Cynthia Toyota

Consultants: Read Jones Christoffersen Consulting Engineers Ltd. (S), MCW Consultants Ltd. (M, E), Ferris + Associates Inc. (L), Curran McCabe Ravindran Ross Inc. (C), Aercoustics Engineering Ltd. (A), Gamsby and Mannerow Engineers (Ci), Eastern Construction (GC)

Computer Science and Engineering Building, Ann Arbor, Michigan
Client: University of Michigan

DSAI Team: Donald Schmitt, David Dow, Duncan Higgins, Michael Lukasik

Walton Chan, Ian Choi, Zvonimir Cicvaric, Charles Gagnon, Dennis Giobbe, Laragh Halldorson, Persis Lam, Jordan Ludington, Dale McDowell, Derek Newby, Mark Ojascastro

Consultants: Read Jones Christoffersen Consulting Engineers Ltd. (S), Crossey Engineering Ltd. (M), Mulvey + Banani International Inc. (E), Vermeulens Cost Consultants (C), Skanska USA Building Inc. (GC)

Country Day School Performing Arts Centre, King City, Ontario
Client: Country Day School

DSAI Team: A.J. Diamond, Jon Soules, Jarle Lovlin

James Blendick, Anna Kogan, Andrea Kordos, Rowana Parker, Don Ryan, Jon Soules, Cynthia Toyota

Consultants: Halcrow Yolles (S), Crossey Engineering Ltd. (M, E), Vermeulens Cost Consultants (C), Novita Limited (T), Aercoustics Engineering Ltd. (A), The Dalton Company (GC)

Davenport Wing, Lash Miller Chemistry Building, Toronto, Ontario
Client: University of Toronto

DSAI Team: Donald Schmitt, Birgit Siber, David Dow, John Featherstone

Kirsten Douglas, Courtenay Henry, Forde Johnson, Gowri Shanker, Chris Stevens, Chloe Town

Consultants: Read Jones Christoffersen Consulting Engineers Ltd. (S), Smith and Andersen Consulting Engineering (M), Crossey Engineering Ltd. (E), Altus Helyar Cost Consulting (C), NXL Architects (La), Bondfield Construction (GC)

Earth Sciences Centre, Toronto, Ontario
Client: University of Toronto

JV Partner: Bregman + Hamann

DSAI Team: Donald Schmitt, Jon Soules, Stewart Adams, George Przybylski

A.J. Diamond, Alison Brooks, Andrew Filarski, Alice Liang, Breck McFarlane, Sandor Rott, Michael Waring

Consultants: Halcrow Yolles (S), TMP Limited (M), Mulvey + Banani International Inc. (E), ENVision: The Hough Group (L), UMA Engineering (GC)

East Bayfront Master Plan Proposal, Toronto, Ontario
Client: Toronto Economic Development Corporation

DSAI Team: A.J. Diamond, Robert Graham

The Esplanade Arts and Heritage Centre, Medicine Hat, Alberta
Client: City of Medicine Hat

JV Partner: Cohos Evamy Integrated Design

DSAI Team: A.J. Diamond, Michael Leckman, Jarle Lovlin

Francesco Bisci, Suzanne Graham, Suzette Lam, Jana Lyskova, Doug Mayr, Harisa Mazgic, Hans Rittmansperger

Consultants: Halcrow Yolles (S), Crossey Engineering Ltd. (M, E), Spiegel Skillen (C), Fisher Dachs Associates (T), Aercoustics Engineering Ltd. (A), AldrichPears Associates (MU), EllisDon (GC)

Evergreen at the Brick Works, Toronto, Ontario
Client: Evergreen

JV Partner: du Toit Allsopp Hillier | Du Toit Architects Limited

DSAI Team: Donald Schmitt, Michael Leckman

Priyanka Bista, Steven Bondar, Walton Chan, Michael Eady

Consultants: Claude Cormier Architectes Paysagistes Inc. (L), ERA Architects (H), Halsall Associates Ltd. (S and LEED), Stantec (M, E), Curran McCabe Ravindran Ross Inc. (C), Leber | Rubes (LS), Ferruccio Sardella (Artist)

Four Seasons Centre for the Performing Arts, Toronto, Ontario
Client: Canadian Opera House Corporation

DSAI Team: A.J. Diamond, Gary McCluskie, Michael Treacy, Matthew Lella, George Przybylski

Duncan Bates, Thomas Caro, Shouheng Chen, Martin Davidson, Tony Diodati, Charles Gagnon, Branka Gazibara, Suzanne Graham, Desmond Gregg, Michele Gucciardi, Kurt Hanzlik, Paddy Harrington, Forde Johnson, Jonathan King, Winga Lam, Gabriel Li, Ana Maria Llanos, Sarah Low, Michael Lukasik, Leo Mieles, Geoff Moote, Farid Noufaily, Hans Rittmansperger, Vladimir Rogojine, Donald Schmitt, Malini Rao Smirnis, Jon Soules, Caroline Spigelski, Goran Sudetic, Eric Sziraki, Adam Thom, Michelle Van Eyk, Sybil Wa, Jessie Waese

Consultants: Halcrow Yolles (S), Crossey Engineering Ltd. (M), Mulvey + Banani International Inc. (E), duToit Allsop Hillier (L), Vermeulens Cost Consultants (C), Fisher Dachs Associates (T), Sound Space Design (A), Aercoustics Engineering Ltd. (A), Engineering Harmonics (A), Wilson, Ihrig & Associates (A), PCL Constructors Canada Inc. (GC)

Garter Lane Arts Centre, Waterford, Ireland
Client: Garter Lane Arts Centre

Associate Architects: Kenneth Wigham Architects, Ireland

DSAI Team: Donald Schmitt, Mike Lukasik, Adam Thom

Consultants: Chris Chapman Associates (S), Crossey Engineering Ltd. (M), Synergy Engineering Ltd. (M), Stewart MacMinn and Partners Co. (E), Theatre Consultants Collaborative, LLC (T)

Gerstein Science Information Centre – Master Plan and Renovations, Toronto, Ontario
Client: University of Toronto

DSAI Team: Donald Schmitt, Gary McCluskie

Stewart Adams, Steve Bondar, Branka Gazibara, Forde Johnson, Ana Maria Llanos, Christina Luk, Bill Rawlings, Chris Stevens, Georgia Ydreos

Consultants: Halcrow Yolles (S), Smith and Andersen Consulting Engineering (M), Mulvey + Banani International Inc. (E), Vermeulens Cost Consultants (C), Michael Thomas Group Inc. (GC), Ryancon General Contractors (GC), Ross Clair Contractors Ltd. (GC), MacViro Consultants (Ci)

Holy Blossom Temple, Toronto, Ontario
Client: Holy Blossom Temple

DSAI Team: A.J. Diamond, Martin Davidson

James Blendick, Dan Gallivan, Breck McFarlane, Farid Noufaily, Graeme Reed, Malini Rao Smirnis

Consultants: Blackwell Bowick Partnership Ltd. (S), Crossey Engineering Ltd. (M, E), Curran McCabe Ravindran Ross Inc. (C), Urban Strategies Inc. (UP)

The Hudson Condominiums, Toronto, Ontario
Client: Great Gulf Homes

DSAI Team: Donald Schmitt, David Dow, Jonathan King

Walton Chan, Brian Kucharski, Persis Lam, Jennifer Mallard, Sony Rai, Susan Tang, Adam Thom, Michael Waring

Consultants: Read Jones Christoffersen Consulting Engineers Ltd. (S), The ECE Group (M, E), NAK Design Group (L), Tucker HiRise Construction Inc. (GC)

Indigo Residence, Mustique, The Grenadines
Client: Mr. and Mrs. Richardson

DSAI Team: A.J. Diamond, Steve Sobel, Michael Szabo

Consultants: Halcrow Yolles (S), G & M Technical Services Ltd. (M, E), Milsom Construction Ltd. (GC)

Integrated Sciences Building, Philadelphia, Pennsylvania
Client: Drexel University

Associate Architects: H2L2 Architects/Planners
DSAI Team: Donald Schmitt, Martin Davidson, Dan Gallivan, Michael Lukasik

John Featherstone, Dennis Giobbe, Martin Kristensen, Rebecca Lai, Persis Lam, Sony Rai, Doug Richardson, Alireza Sherafati, Peggy Theodore

Consultants: Halcrow Yolles (S), Keast & Hood Co. (S), Crossey Engineering Ltd. (M, E), International Consultants (C), Gilbane Building Co. (GC), Stantec (Ci)

The Israeli Ministry of Foreign Affairs, Jerusalem, Israel
Client: Foreign Ministry Israel

Associate Architects: Kolker, Kolker, Epstein Architects

DSAI Team: A.J. Diamond, Jon Soules, George Przybylski

Suzanne Graham, Anna Kogan, Martin Russocki, Birgit Siber, Caroline Spigelski, Mike Szabo, Peggy Theodore

Consultants: Yaron-Shimoni-Shacham Consulting Engineers Ltd. (S), The Mitchell Partnership, Inc. (M), Shapira-Hahn Consulting Engineers Ltd. (M), Amnon Yosha Consulting Engineers (Plumbing), Itkin Blum Electrical Engineering (E), Ronit Soen (Lighting), Yoav Aldaag (Fire and Life Safety), Darrell A. Chivu Inc. (Curtain Wall Consultant), E. Rahat and Associates (Construction Managers), Arenson Ltd. (GC)

Jerusalem City Hall, Jerusalem, Israel
Client: City of Jerusalem

JV Partner/Associate Architects: Kolker, Kolker, Epstein Architects, Bogod Figuerido, Niv Krendall

DSAI Team: A.J. Diamond, Mary Jane Finlayson, Martin Davidson, Catherine Benotto

David Hileman, Avi Rosenburg, Donald Schmitt

Consultants: Yaron-Shimoni-Shacham Consulting Engineers Ltd. (S), Multivision Electrosonic Limited (M), G. Itkin E. Blum Electrical Engineering Ltd. (E), Ron Construction (GC)

The Jewish Community Center in Manhattan, New York, New York
Client: Jewish Community Center

Associate Architects: Schuman Lichtenstein Claman Efron Architects

DSAI Team: A.J. Diamond, Martin Davidson, Pat Hanson, George Przybylski

Gregory Colucci, Desmond Gregg, Pat Hanson, Jarle Lovin, Leo Mieles, Donald Schmitt, Peggy Theodore

Consultants: DeSimone Consulting Engineers (S), Lehr Consultants International (M, E), AMEC (GC)

Leggatt Hall and Watts Hall, Kingston, Ontario
Client: Queens University

JV Partner: Shoalts & Zaback Architects Ltd.
DSAI Team: Donald Schmitt, Michael Lukasik, Donna Dolan
Cecilia Chen, Brian Kucharski, Florin Tanasoiu, Adam Thom

Consultants: Halcrow Yolles (S), Smith and Anderson Consulting Engineering (M), Stantec (E), Ferris + Associates Ltd. (L), Aecon Buildings (GC)

Legislative Assembly of Ontario – Renovation Master Plan and Implementation, Toronto, Ontario
Client: Legislative Assembly of Ontario

Associate Architects: Shoalts & Zaback Architects Ltd.

DSAI Team: Donald Schmitt, Martin Donaldson, Stewart Adams, Jon Soules

Branka Gazibara, Courtney Henry, Pat Hanson, Gowri Shanker, Steve Sobel, Adam Thom, Mike Yuen

Consultants: Halcrow Yolles (s), Smith and Andersen Consulting Engineers (M), Mulvey + Banani International Inc. (E), Vermeulens Cost Consultants (C), Vanbots Construction Corporation and Buttcon Limited (GC)

Li Ka Shing Knowledge Institute, Toronto, Ontario
Client: St. Michael's Hospital

DSAI Team: A.J. Diamond, Paul Szaszkiewicz, Matt Smith

Steve Bondar, Robert Boyd, Aaron Costain, Jamie Duncan, Michael Eady, John Featherstone, Michael Fok, Vincent Goetz, Jim Graves, Desmond Gregg, Bruce Han, Matthew Hague, Martin Kristensen, Dale McDowell, Breck McFarlane, Adrian Politano, Robin Ramcharan, Doug Richardson, Kevin Rodger, Antra Roze, Cristian Simonescu, Jessie Waese

Consultants: Carruthers & Wallace Ltd. (S), H.H. Angus & Associates Ltd. (M, E), Ferris + Associates Inc. (L), Vermeulens Cost Consultants (C), Aercoustics Engineering Ltd. (A), Eastern Construction (GC)

Life Sciences Centre, Vancouver, British Columbia
Client: University of British Columbia

JV Partner: Bunting Coady Architects

DSAI Team: A.J. Diamond, Paul Szaszkiewicz, John Featherstone, Peggy Theodore

Desmond Gregg, Michele Gucciardi, Geoffrey Hodgetts, Martin Kristensen, Alan Ng, Sony Rai, Bill Rawlings, Graeme Reed, Gary Watson, Ed Weinberg

Consultants: Read Jones Christoffersen Consulting Engineers Ltd. (S), MCW Consultants Ltd. (M, E), Resource Planning Group (La), Aercoustics Engineering Ltd. (A), Phillips Farevaag Smallenberg (L), Alpin Martin Consultants Ltd. (C), Ledcor Construction Limited (GC)

Life Sciences Complex, Montreal, Quebec
Client: McGill University

JV Partner: Provencher Roy + Associés Architectes

DSAI Team: A.J. Diamond, Paul Szaszkiewicz, Caroline Spigelski

John Featherstone, Michele Gucciardi, Martin Kristensen, Breck McFarlane, Graeme Reed, Jesse Waese

Consultants: Saia Deslauriers Kadanoff (S), Pageau Morel et Associés Inc. (M, E), Claude Cormier Architectes Paysagistes Inc. (L), Pomerleau Inc. (GC)

Los Alamos Civic Center, Los Alamos, New Mexico
Client: County of Los Alamos

DSAI Team: Donald Schmitt, Jon Soules, Michael Leckman

Derek Newby, Jessie Waese

Consultants: Chavez-Grieves Consulting Engineers Inc. (S), Bridgers & Paxton Consulting Engineers Inc. (M, E), Morrow Reardon Wilkinson Miller, Ltd. (L), Balis & Co. (C), Fisher Dachs Associates (T), Jaffe Holden Acoustics Inc. (A)

Maria Shchuka District Branch Library, Toronto, Ontario
Client: Toronto Public Library

DSAI Team: Donald Schmitt, Sarah Low, Peggy Theodore

Ivana Gazic, Forde Johnson, Frank Mazzulla, Jo Palma, Diana Saragosa, Birgit Siber

Consultants: Blackwell Bowick Partnership Ltd. (S), Hidi Rae Consulting Engineering Inc. (M, E), Gunta Mackars Landscape Architecture (L), Altus Helyar Cost Consulting (C), Van Horne Construction (GC), Aercoustics Engineering Ltd. (A)

Marion McCain Faculty of Arts and Social Sciences Building, Halifax, Nova Scotia
Client: Dalhousie University

JV Partner/Associate Architects: Lydon Lynch Architects Limited
DSAI Team: A.J. Diamond, Michael Szabo

Suzanne Graham, Seth Isnar, Anna Kogan, Chris Stevens

Consultants: Campbell, Comeau Engineering Ltd. (S), Morris & Richard Consulting Engineers, Ltd. (M, E), Reinhart L. Petersmann Landscape Architects (L), Hanscomb Associates (C), Atlantic Acoustical Associates (A), Dalhousie Services Ltd. (GC)

Max M. Fisher Music Center, Detroit, Michigan
Client: Detroit Symphony Orchestra

Associate Architects: Gunn Levine Architects
DSAI Team: Donald Schmitt, Antra Roze, Kevin Weiss

Mark Berest, Francesco Bisci, Peter Brigden, Sydney Browne, Terry Cecil, Gregory Colucci, Donna Dolan, Dan Gallivan, Robin Glover, Suzanne Graham, Desmond Gregg, Courtenay Henry, Kai Hesse, Theo Kelaiditis, Ana Maria Llanos, Jerel Loponen, Jennifer Mallard, Breck McFarlane, Jo Palma, Ajit Rao, Don Ryan, Florin Tanasoiu, Cynthia Toyota

Consultants: Halcrow Yolles (S), CEL International (M, E), Donnell Consultants Inc. (C), Curran McCabe Ravindran Ross Inc. (C), Schuler Shook (T), JaffeHolden Acoustics (A), George W. Auch Company (GC)

Medical Education Building, Windsor, Ontario
Client: University of Windsor

JV Partner/Associate Architects: DiMaio Design Associates | Architect Inc.

DSAI Team: Donald Schmitt, Caroline Spigelski

Duncan Bates, Jessica Cheung, Mark Cichy, Desmond Gregg, Diana Saragosa, Cristian Simonescu

Consultants: Halcrow Yolles (S), Crossey Engineering Ltd. (M, E), Curran McCabe Ravindran Ross Inc. (C), Ferris + Associates Inc. (L), Oscar Construction Company Limited (GC)

Memorial Pool, Toronto (Etobicoke), Ontario
Client: City of Toronto (West District)

JV Partner/Associate Architects: G. Bruce Stratton Architects

DSAI Team: Donald Schmitt, Gary McCluskie

Tania Bortolotto, Seth Isnar, Gowri Shanker, Mike Szabo

Consultants: Halcrow Yolles (S), Ellard-Wilson Engineering Ltd. (M, E), Gunta Mackars Landscape Architecture (L), The Atlas Corporation (GC)

Metro Central YMCA, Toronto, Ontario
Client: YMCA

DSAI Team: A.J. Diamond, Donald Schmitt, Vic Jaunkalns, Derek Revington, Jon Soules

Rick Andrighetti, Douglas Birkenshaw, Sherry Blake, Grant Diemert, Dino Dutra, Pat Hanson, Sandra McKee, Sharon McKenzie, Brenda Millar, Michael Morrisey, Val Rynimeri, Anne Sinclair, David Weir

Consultants: Halcrow Yolles (S), The ECE Group Ltd. (M, E), Vermeulens Cost Consultants (C), Mollenhauer Ltd. (GC)

Minto Lonsdale Condominiums, Toronto, Ontario
Client: MintoUrban Communities

DSAI Team: Donald Schmitt, Graeme Reed

Gary Chien, Mark Cichy, Bruce Han, Jon Soules, Elcin Yeter, Joe Zingaro

Consultants: ERA Architects (H), Urban Strategies (UP), Walker, Nott, Dragicevic Associates Ltd. (UP), Phillips Farevaag Smallenberg (L), Al Underhill & Associates Ltd. (Ci)

New Brunswick Museum, Saint John, New Brunswick
Client: New Brunswick Museum

Associate Architects: Murdock & Boyd Architects

DSAI Team: A.J. Diamond, Michael Leckman

Priyanka Bista, Walton Chan, Jessica Liefl, Graeme Reed, Birgit Siber, Cristian Simonescu, Jon Soules, David Stone, Ted Teng, Peggy Theodore, Cynthia Toyota

Consultants: CBCL Ltd. (S), Tweedie & Associates (M), Ralph Smith Engineering Inc. (E), BDA Ltd. Landscape Architects (L), Curran McCabe Ravindran Ross Inc. (C), Lord Cultural Resources (MU)

Ontario Science Centre – Master Plan and Renovations, Toronto, Ontario
Client: Ontario Science Centre

DSAI Team: A.J. Diamond, Gary McCluskie

Sydney Browne, Walton Chan, Robert Labonte, Hilary Pinnington, Sarah Schuele

Consultants: Halcrow Yolles (S), Crossey Engineering Ltd. (M, E), Curran McCabe Ravindran Ross Inc. (C), Buttcon Limited (GC)

Pierre Berton Resource Library, Vaughan, Ontario
Client: Vaughan Public Libraries

DSAI Team: Gary McCluskie, Jennifer Mallard

Jennifer Anderson, Graham Gavine, Forde Johnson, Edward Kim, Vladimir Rogojine, Donald Schmitt

Consultants: Blackwell Bowick Partnership Ltd. (S),Crossey Engineering Ltd. (M, E), Janet Rosenberg + Associates (L), Vermeulens Cost Consultants (C), Maystar General Contractors (GC)

Regent Park Community Health Centre, Toronto, Ontario
Client: Regent Park Community Health Centre

DSAI Team: A.J. Diamond, Stewart Adams

Gowri Shanker, Chris Stevens, Peggy Theodore, Mike Yuen

Consultants: Blackwell Bowick Partnership Ltd.(S), Smith and Anderson Consulting Engineering (M), Mulvey + Banani International Inc. (E), Richard & B.A. Ryan Limited (GC)

Richmond Hill Central Library, Richmond Hill, Ontario
Client: Town of Richmond Hill

DSAI Team: A.J. Diamond, Gary McCluskie, George Friedman, Stewart Adams

Dalibor Cizek, Stuart Feldman, David Hileman, Jennifer Stanley, Mike Yuen

Consultants: Halsall Engineering (S), Crossey Engineering Ltd. (M, E), Vermeulens Cost Consultants (C), Buttcon Limited (GC)

School of Computer Science and Engineering, Jerusalem, Israel
Client: The Hebrew University of Jerusalem

JV Partner/Associate Architects: Kolker, Kolker, Epstein Architects

DSAI Team: A.J. Diamond, Jon Soules, Dan Klinck

Stephen Bondar, Atsunobu Maeda

Consultants: Ephraim Cohen Civil Engineer (S), Eitan Harvel (M), Rafael Cohen (E), Ronit Soen (Lighting), Rachelle Wiener (L)

School of Image Arts, Toronto, Ontario
Client: Ryerson University

DSAI Team: Donald Schmitt, Peggy Theodore

Liviu Budur, Kevin Rodger, Andreas Sokolowski

Consultants: Halcrow Yolles (S), Crossey Engineering Ltd. (M, E), Curran McCabe Ravindran Ross Inc. (C), Consullux (Lighting)

Sidney Harman Hall, Washington, District of Columbia
Client: The Shakespeare Theater Company

DSAI Team: A.J. Diamond, Gary McCluskie, Jennifer Mallard

Liana Bresler, Walton Chan, Dan Gallivan, Michael Feinberg, Alexander Josephson, Dan Klinck, Martin Kristensen, Jana Lyskova, Petra Muenzel, Greg Perkins, Antra Roze, Goran Sudetic, Cynthia Toyota, Michael Treacy, Joe Zingaro

Consultants: Crossey Engineering Ltd. (M), Mulvey + Banani International Inc. (E), Fisher Dachs Associates (T), Talaske (A)
Office Tower/Base Building Architects: SmithGroup Inc.

Office Tower/Base Building Consultants: Tadjer-Cohen-Edelson-Associates Inc. (S), Girard Engineering (M, E), Wiles Mensch Corp. (Ci), Clark Construction (GC)

Southbrook Vineyards, Niagara-on-the-Lake, Ontario
Client: Southbrook Winery

DSAI Team: A.J. Diamond, Martin Davidson, Walton Chan

James Blendick, Malini Rao Smirnis, Cynthia Toyota

Consultants: Blackwell Bowick Partnership Ltd. (S), Crossey Engineering Ltd. (M, E), du Toit Allsopp Hillier (L), Merit Contractors (GC)

Student Centre, Toronto, Ontario
Client: York University

DSAI Team: A.J. Diamond, Phillip Beesley, Michael Leckman

Marie Black, Dalibor Cizek, Stewart Feldman, Anne-Marie Flemming, George Friedman, Courtenay Henry

Consultants: Read Jones Christoffersen Consulting Engineers Ltd. (S), Merber Corporation (M), Stantec (E)

Susur Restaurant, Toronto, Ontario
Client: Susur Lee

DSAI Team: Gregory Colucci
Joy Fogg, Chris Stevens

Consultants: Blackwell Bowick Partnership Ltd. (S), G & M Technical Services Ltd. (M, E), Paul Mathieson (Lighting), Marcus Design Build Inc. (GC)

TEDCO's Corus Building, Toronto, Ontario
Client: Toronto Economic Development Corporation

DSAI Team: A.J. Diamond, David Dow, Jon Soules, Antra Roze, Matthew Lella

Robert Boyd, Jed Braithwait, Gary Chien, Chris Clarke, Zvonimir Cicvaric, Vincent Goetz, Desmond Gregg, Bruce Han, Duncan Higgins, Forde Johnson, Dan Klinck, Giuseppe Mandarino, Ping Pai, Diana Saragosa, Michael Waring, Coco Keyu Xiong, Elcin Yeter

Consultants: Halcrow Yolles (S), Smith and Anderson Consulting Engineering (M), Stantec (E), Aercoustics Engineering Ltd., (A), Altus Helyar Cost Consulting (C), Enermodal Engineering (LEED)

Thayer Building, Ann Arbor, Michigan
Client: University of Michigan

DSAI Team: Donald Schmitt, Thom Pratt, Malini Rao Smirnis

Aaron Costain, Donna Dolan, Dan Gallivan, Robert Labonte, Ines Marchese, Harisa Mazgic,

Consultants: Read Jones Christoffersen Consulting Engineers Ltd. (S), Crossey Engineering Ltd. (M, E), Vermeulens Cost Consultants Inc. (C), Walbridge Aldinger Company (GC)

University of Guelph-Humber Building, Toronto, Ontario
Client: Humber College/University of Guelph

JV Partner: Rieder, Hymmen & Lobban Architects Inc.

DSAI Team: Donald Schmitt, Birgit Siber, John Featherstone

Michaele Gucciardi, Agnes Kazmierczak, Martin Kristensen, Persis Lam, Malini Rao Smirnis, Cynthia Toyota

Consultants: Halcrow Yolles (S), Crossey Engineering Ltd. Ltd. (M, E), Peter Owen (L), Aercoustics Engineering Ltd. (A), Ball Construction (GC)

University of Ontario Institute of Technology – Campus and Buildings, Oshawa, Ontario
Client: University of Ontario Institute for Technology

DSAI Team: Donald Schmitt, Michael Szabo, Mark Berest, Sydney Browne, Donna Dolan, Matthew Smith

Christian Alkins, Duncan Bates, Stephen Bauer, Frank Bisci, James Blendick, Steven Bondar, Cecilia Chen, Shouheng Chen, Elena Chernyshov, Steven Choe, Mark Cichy, Miklos Conti, Aaron Costain, Leonardo de Melo, Charlotte Dunfield, Kent Eliuk, John Featherstone, John Robert Feeney, Miriam Fitzpatrick, Joy Fogg, Charles Gagnon, Rick Galezowski, Graham Gavine,

Vincent Goetz, Michele Gucciardi, Lisa Hasan, Duncan Higgins, Bryan Jin, Agnes Kazmierczak, Edward Kim, Jonathan King, Dan Klinck, Meldan Kutertan, Robert Labonte, Andrea Lacalamnita, Suzette Lam, Gabriel Li, Sarah Low, Jana Lyskova, Warren Mack, Carl Madsen, Atsunobu Maeda, Ines Marchese, Harisa Mazgic, Gary McCluskie, Breck McFarlane, Derek Newby, Farid Noufaily, Yekta Pakdaman-Hamedani, Neal Panchuk, Ian Pieterse, Doug Richardson, Vladimir Rogojine, Don Ryan, Birgit Siber, Malini Rao Smirnis, Steve Sobel, Kristin Speth, Michael Szabo, Florin Tanasoiu, Michael Waring, Joe Zingaro

Consultants: Halcrow Yolles (S), Stantec (M, E), Crossey Engineering Ltd. (M, E), duToit Allsopp Hillier (L), Schollen & Company (L), Vermeulens Cost Consultants (C), EllisDon (GC)

Urban Block Redevelopment, Regent Park, Toronto, Ontario
Client: Toronto Community Housing Corporation

Associate Architects: Graziani + Corazza Architects

DSAI Team: Donald Schmitt, Robert Boyd, Jonathan King , Ana Maria Llanos, Paul Mezei, Bernd Mueller, Goran Sudetic, Karl Van Es, Elcin Yeter

Consultants: Sigmund Soudack & Associates (S), LKM Consulting (M, E), NAK Design Group (L)

Ways Lane, Toronto, Ontario
Client: Claire Ironside

DSAI Team: Donald Schmitt, Courtenay Henry

Consultants: Halcrow Yolles (S), Ed Gaigalas (GC)

STAFF LIST

Principals

Gregory Colucci
Martin Davidson
A.J. Diamond
David Dow
Robert Graham
Helen Kabriel
Michael Leckman
Gary McCluskie
Thom Pratt
Donald Schmitt
Birgit Siber
Jon Soules
Michael Szabo
Paul Szaszkiewicz

Associates

Sydney Browne
John Featherstone
Branka Gazibara
Matthew Lella
Ana Maria Llanos
Jarle Lovlin
Michael Lukasik
Jennifer Mallard
Antra Roze
Matthew Smith
Caroline Spigelski
Peggy Theodore
Michael Treacy

Jennifer Anderson
Duncan Bates
Teresa Bayani
Christine Bellerby
Priyanka Bista
James Blendick
Steven Bondar
Scott Bouwmeester
Robert Boyd
Liviu Budur
Luciana Budur
Christian Burgsthaler
Cynthia Carbonneau
Walton F. Chan
Abubakar Chowdhury
Mark Cichy
Zvonimir Cicvaric
Christopher Clarke
Joshua Cohen
Aaron Costain
Leonardo De Melo
Donna Dolan
Michael Donaldson
Kirsten Douglas
Jamie Duncan
Kent Eliuk
Kate Featherstone
Dan Gallivan
Calin Gibea
Dennis Giobbe
Vincent Goetz
Jim Graves
Desmond Gregg
Elizabeth Gyde
Bruce (Qingmin) Han
Duncan Higgins
Forde Johnson
Agnieszka Kazmierczak
Deena Kiproff
Dan Klinck
Martin Kristensen
Jan Ladisich
Persis Lam

Janouque LeRiche
Nisha Lewis
Catherine Lin
Sarah Low
Eric Lucassen
Giuseppe Mandarino
Michelle Matthews
Dale McDowell
Breck McFarlane
Trevor McNaughton
Leo Mieles
Ryan Mitchell
Thomas Nemeskeri
Yekta Pakdaman
Jeanette Parker
Gregory Perkins
Tara Plett
Sony Satinder Rai
Graeme Reed
Doug Richardson
Kevin Rodger
Utra Samlal-Ramlakhan
Diana Saragosa
Shelley Sebastian
Chen Shalita
Sonja Shuffler
Lillian Sillaots
Malini Rao Smirnis
Andreas Sokolowski
Nigel Tai
Regina Thian
Stephanie Town
Cynthia Toyota
Giselle Tucker
Katya Tunon-Marshall
Theressa Valmonte
Kris Vassilev
Sarah Vowell
Jessica Waese
Michael Waring
Gary Watson
Kristy Wung
Elcin Yeter
Javier Zeller
Shenshu Zhang
Joe Zingaro
Sheva Zohouri

The firm has grown from that of a single proprietor with two employees in the 1970s to an incorporated company with fourteen principals, thirteen associates and a staff compliment of over 130 people in 2008.

Notwithstanding the significant changes in the size of office and the scope of the work – the firm is working worldwide – a consistent set of operating principles has remained in place throughout the firm's history. The aim of these principles has been to maintain the collaborative, mutually supportive, and participatory practice for all members of the firm.

This has been accomplished by meetings of the principals and associates to discuss and formulate policy and strategy. Committees covering each aspect of the practice, chaired by a principal or associate, develop position papers for debate and resolution by the principals.

A longstanding tradition of the firm is its Friday afternoon review. The entire office is invited (with beer and popcorn at hand) to participate in the critique of projects presented to the office. Every project is subject to such scrutiny. The discourse – read, at times, argument – about the projects is often enlightening, producing fresh insights, useful comments and in general alternative perspectives on the work. Projects have been known to change direction from such useful review. It is also, at times, the best seminar on architecture.

Perhaps the most unusual practice is soup-making. Members of the office make soup once or twice a year. The intention is to facilitate informal meeting and collegial discussion. Given that twenty-seven languages are spoken in the office, the recipes are sometimes wild and certainly varied. We intend to produce a DSAI soup recipe book!

A consequence of both our design strength (over 140 national and international awards) and our inclusive management style, a panel of the Queen's University School of Business, KPMG, Deloitte and the Canadian Imperial Bank of Commerce included the firm as one of the 50 Best Managed Companies in Canada 2004, the first architectural firm with this distinction.

BIOGRAPHIES

A.J. DIAMOND

A.J. Diamond's degrees include a Bachelor of Architecture (with distinction) from the University of Capetown, a Master of Arts in politics, philosophy and economics from Oxford University and a Master of Architecture from the University of Pennsylvania. He was the first occupant of the Graham Chair at Penn, established for those who have successfully combined theory and practice in architecture.

He is a Fellow of the Royal Architectural Institute of Canada and the Canadian Institute of Planners and an Honourary Fellow of the American Institute of Architects. He has received honourary doctorates in Engineering from DalTech and in Law from the University of Toronto. He is a Royal Architectural Institute of Canada Gold Medalist, a member of the Order of Ontario and an Officer of the Order of Canada.

Mr. Diamond was instrumental in the movement to reinforce neighbourhoods at risk with infill housing; he devised medium-rise alternatives at equivalent densities to high-rise residential development; as an entrepreneur he demonstrated the economic effectiveness of recycling historic structures for new uses; and he identified the negative impacts of suburban sprawl.

Extra professional activities include chairmanship of the Advisory Committee on Design to the Canadian National Capital Commission, membership of the Ontario Human Rights Commission, a role as a commissioner of the Greater Toronto Area Task Force, which made recommendations on governance, taxation, land-use planning and transportation for the GTA. Three exhibitions have been held of his travel sketches and paintings. His lecture tours have included Australia, New Zealand, the United Kingdom, South Africa and Italy.

DONALD SCHMITT

Born in South Porcupine, Ontario, Donald Schmitt is a graduate of the University of Toronto Schools and the Faculty of Architecture, University of Toronto. He was awarded the Royal Architectural Institute of Canada Medal in the thesis year. He has been Adjunct Professor at the Faculty of Architecture, University of Toronto, and Adjunct Professor and External Examiner, the School of Architecture, Dalhousie University. He has also been a guest lecturer and visiting critic at various Canadian and American universities, including the University of Texas, University of Pennsylvania, University of Michigan, University of Waterloo and the University of British Columbia.

He is the founding chair of the Public Art Commission for the City of Toronto, for which he was awarded the Civic Medal. He is currently a member of the Advisory Committee on Planning Design and Real Estate for the National Capital Commission, Ottawa, and a member of the Waterfront Toronto Design Review Panel.

He is a Fellow of the Royal Architectural Institute of Canada, a member of the Architects Associations of Ontario, Alberta, British Columbia and Nova Scotia, a member of the American Institute of Architects and a board member of the Canadian Art Foundation.

GREGORY COLUCCI A member of the firm since 1988, Gregory Colucci has coordinated the design and implementation of numerous large projects, particularly in health care, recreation and resort residential developments overseas. While completing a Bachelor of Architecture degree at Carleton University in 1982, he spent his fourth year of study at the Unité Pédagogique d'Architecture no. 4 in Paris. He is bilingual in French and English and holds a Bachelor of Arts with a major in Art History. Gregory was project architect for the award-winning Baycrest Centre for Geriatric Care, Apotex Centre, Toronto, and Cawthra Community Centre, Mississauga. Recently he has directed significant residential and hotel developments in Bulgaria and the Russian Federation.

MARTIN DAVIDSON In his twenty years with the firm, Martin Davidson has established himself as being particularly expert in both historic renovation and new construction. From his early work on Jerusalem City Hall and as project architect for the JCC in Manhattan and the renovations to the Legislative Assembly of Ontario, he has distinguished himself on institutional buildings of varying scale and complexity. Currently he is the project architect for Holy Blossom Temple and School in Toronto, Southbrook Vineyards in Niagara-on-the-Lake and the new Instructional Laboratory Building at Drexel University in Philadelphia, all projects with a strong sustainable design focus.

Serving on the Executive of the Toronto Society of Architects for several years, Martin was responsible for a wide-ranging series of initiatives, including the institution of the Fellowship Award Program, the TSA film and lecture series, and exhibitions by national and international architects. He has also represented the architectural community on urban design issues, serving as the TSA representative to the City of Toronto on the development of urban design guidelines.

DAVID DOW With a Bachelor of Science in Architecture from the University of Dundee, Scotland, and a Bachelor of Architecture from the University of Waterloo, David Dow brings considerable design expertise to architectural projects of varying complexity and size. Since joining Diamond and Schmitt Architects in 1999, he has worked on a range of institutional and health-care projects, including St. Michael's Hospital Victoria Wing Addition, the Bahen Centre for Information Technology at the University of Toronto, the Hudson Condominiums building in Toronto and the Computer Science and Engineering Building at the University of Michigan. Currently, David is the project architect for TEDCO's Corus Building, the new headquarters for Corus Entertainment.

ROBERT GRAHAM Joining Diamond and Schmitt Architects in 1997, Robert Graham has worked on a variety of institutional and development projects. With a degree in Environmental Studies from the University of Waterloo's School of Urban and Regional Planning, he directs feasibility studies, urban design and project planning exercises. Robert is the lead on a consultant consortium developing a 15-hectare brownfield site in Hamilton. The McMaster Innovation Park master plan will guide development for 83,600 square metres of research-based industry over the next 20 years. He also manages the business development and marketing group for Diamond and Schmitt Architects.

HELEN KABRIEL Since joining Diamond and Schmitt Architects in 1998 as comptroller, Helen Kabriel has been instrumental in guiding the firm through a period of significant and complex growth. A graduate of the University of Western Ontario, she also received a post-graduate degree in Commerce from the University of Windsor. With professional experience in banking, office procedures and project management, she has focused exclusively on architectural accounting since 1985. Helen's knowledge and expertise have provided Diamond and Schmitt Architects with a strong business foundation on which the firm has been able to expand. In 2001, she received the highest achievement award available from the Society of Design Administration Canada. Helen has been on the executive committee of Canstruction since its inception in 1988. She is currently the co-chair for this charitable competition, which creates large structures out of thousands of cans of food by teams from the design industry, the proceeds of which then go to the local food bank.

MICHAEL LECKMAN Michael Leckman was inspired to join Diamond and Schmitt Architects in 1977, after a season of performances in the Citadel Theatre in Edmonton. His start with the firm was much later, in 1988, and his first project – the York University Student Centre – won a Governor General's Award for Architecture. Since then, he has been project architect for buildings in Ontario, New Brunswick, Alberta, British Columbia and New Mexico, has been a frequent guest critic, instructor and speaker at schools of architecture, and is a member of the City of Toronto's new design review panel. His list of key assignments also includes the Bahen Centre at the University of Toronto, the Esplanade in Medicine Hat, the Sheridan College Centre for Advanced Manufacturing, the Los Alamos Civic Center, and the New Brunswick Museum. Currently he is working on a hotel in Barrie, Ontario, and the redevelopment of Toronto's Don Valley Brick Works into a centre for environmental education.

THOM PRATT A graduate of the University of Toronto School of Architecture, Thom Pratt joined Diamond and Schmitt Architects in 1986. Since then, his work has focused on institutional buildings in both the public and private sectors. His project experience includes renovations to IBM's Canadian headquarters in Markham, the Salvation Army's City Core project in downtown Toronto and the Bahen Centre for Information Technology at the University of Toronto. Currently, Thom is the project architect for the master plan and implementation of projects at three campuses of Mohawk College. He chairs the computer and technology committee at Diamond and Schmitt Architects.

GARY MCCLUSKIE Gary McCluskie is a graduate of the School of Architecture at the University of Waterloo, where he received a Bachelor of Environmental Studies and Bachelor of Architecture. In over twenty years with the firm, he has developed design expertise in cultural, institutional, and residential building types, with a focus on assembly buildings and public spaces. He was the managing principal for both the Four Seasons Centre for the Performing Arts in Toronto and Sidney Harman Hall in Washington, D.C. Many of his projects have been recognized with design awards, including a Governor General's Award for the Richmond Hill Central Library and Awards of Excellence from the Ontario Association of

Architects for the Etobicoke Memorial Pool, the University of Toronto Gerstein Library and Four Seasons Centre. In 2005, the American Library Association recognized the Pierre Berton Resource Library as the best public library in North America. Gary has been a visiting critic at the University of Toronto and the University of Waterloo. He has participated in the design of public art and his winning entry for *Ecolage* blended sustainable design and public art for an installation focused on the regeneration of the lower Don River in Toronto.

BIRGIT SIBER Birgit Siber was born in Montreal and educated at the University of Toronto, where she received the Lieutenant Governor's Award for architecture in her thesis year. Joining Diamond and Schmitt Architects in 1996, she brings considerable architectural and design expertise to the firm. Birgit has contributed to numerous award-winning projects, including the Foreign Ministry in Jerusalem. In the role of project architect, she has focused on a broad range of institutional and laboratory projects, including the Lash Miller Chemistry Lab and University of Guelph-Humber, which incorporates the first innovative bio-filter plant wall. Her master plan projects include the Mount Allison Campus master plan, the University of Windsor Engineering master plan, and The Michener Institute master plan and renovation. Sustainability has been a leitmotif in Birgit's work; she co-chairs the office sustainable design committee and actively promotes green building design within the office and the community. She is currently focused on the design of the CANMET Building, a materials testing laboratory for the federal government with a LEED Platinum target.

JON SOULES Jon Soules attended the Ontario College of Art and graduated from the University of Waterloo School of Architecture, where he won the Royal Architectural Institute of Canada Medal for Design. He has taught at the University of Waterloo and the University of Toronto. He was project architect for the Israeli Foreign Ministry in Jerusalem, winner of the 2004 Business Week/ Architectural Record Award, the Country Day School Performing Arts Centre and the Junior School Gymnasium in King Township, the Canadian Chancery in Prague, the Hebrew University School of Engineering and Computer Science in Jerusalem and the National Arts Centre Theatre renovations. His current projects include the Country Day School Fitness Centre, the new headquarters for Corus Entertainment on Toronto's waterfront and the new offices and medical operating theatres for the Clearview Institute in Toronto. An accomplished artist, he won American Society of Architectural Illustrators Awards of Excellence in 2006, 2007 and 2008.

MICHAEL SZABO Joining Diamond and Schmitt in 1994, Michael Szabo brings a broad range of experience to the firm, including the master planning and design of medium- and high-density residential apartments and special-needs housing. He has completed an array of institutional, recreational, and academic projects with the firm working on the Creative Arts Facility at the University of British Columbia and the award-winning Marion McCain Faculty of Arts and Sciences Building at Dalhousie University. With his extensive experience in undergraduate and graduate research laboratories and academic design, Michael is currently project principal for the $440 million campus buildings, and master plan at the University of Ontario Institute of Technology (UOIT). Designed as a model sustainable academic community the UOIT master plan encompasses the development of a 17-hectare campus including 83,600 square metres of gross floor area. This innovative project has won an RAIC award, a SCUP award for campus design, an American library design award, and was presented by Michael at the 2006 USGBC Greenbuild Conference on sustainable campus design.

PAUL SZASZKIEWICZ Paul Szaszkiewicz holds a Bachelor of Environmental Science and a Bachelor of Architecture from the University of Waterloo, and joined Diamond and Schmitt Architects in 1996. He is a member of the OAA and the RAIC, and has been a principal of Diamond and Schmitt Architects since 2003. Paul has assembled, managed and led large design teams for a number of the firm's largest institutional health and research projects. Notable projects include the UBC Life Sciences Centre, which was awarded the USGBC LEED Gold Certification, the Cardinal Carter Wing and the Li Ka Shing Knowledge Institute for St. Michael's Hospital, and the Bellini Pavilion and Cancer Research Centre for McGill University. Paul also led teams for the City of North Vancouver's Block 62 mixed-use master plan and for the design of their new central library and civic plaza. He is a frequent speaker at academic research conferences and participated as a Canadian Change Foundation healthcare study tour delegate to Norway and Sweden in 2007.

AWARDS

2007

Four Seasons Centre for the Performing Arts, Toronto
BusinessWeek / Architectural Record Award
Citation for Excellence

Toronto Urban Design Award
Public Building in Context - Award of Excellence
Award of Excellence

Building Magazine
Outside the Box Award - Architecturally
Innovative Design

Ontario Association of Architects
Design Excellence Award

Toronto Central Waterfront
Toronto Urban Design Award
Vision and Master Plan - Award of Excellence

Centre for Manufacturing and Design Technologies, Sheridan College, Davis Campus, Brampton
Building Magazine
Outside the Box Award - Architecturally
Innovative Design

University of Ontario Institute of Technology, Oshawa
Building Magazine
Outside the Box Award - Green Building Design

Los Alamos Civic Center, New Mexico
American Institute of Architects
Western Mountain Region Awards - Merit Award

The Esplanade - Medicine Hat Performing Arts and Heritage Centre, Medicine Hat
Canadian Consulting Engineering Awards
Schreyer Award for Acoustic Design

Pierre Berton Resource Library, Vaughan
The Ontario Library Association
Award of Excellence

New Brunswick Museum, St. John
American Society of Architectural Illustrators
Architecture in Perspective 22 Awards

2006

Four Seasons Centre for the Performing Arts, Toronto
The Brick Industry Association
Brick in Architecture Awards - Best in Class

Ontario Concrete Awards
Structural Design Innovation Award

Centre for Manufacturing and Design Technologies, Sheridan College, Davis Campus, Brampton
Ontario Concrete Awards
Sustainable Concrete Construction

The Esplanade - Medicine Hat Performing Arts and Heritage Centre, Medicine Hat
The Brick Industry Association
Brick in Architecture Awards - Silver

University of Ontario Institute of Technology, Oshawa
Society of College and University Planning /
American Institute of Architects Committee on

Architecture for Education
Honor Award for Excellence in Planning for a
New Campus

Canadian Society of Landscape Architects
Regional Honour Award

Library, University of Ontario Institute of Technology, Oshawa
American Library Association / International
Interior Design Association
Library Interior Design Competition
Honor Award - Academic Library
Best of Show

Pierre Berton Resource Library, Vaughan
American Library Association / International
Interior Design Association
Library Interior Design Competition
Honor Award - Public Library

Toronto Waterfront Study
American Society of Architectural Illustrators
Architecture in Perspective 21 Awards

Life Sciences Building, University of British Columbia
US Green Building Council (USGBC)
Leadership in Energy and Environmental Design
(LEED®) Gold certification

Building Magazine
Outside the box Award - Green Building Design

2005

Los Alamos Civic Centre, New Mexico
Canadian Architect Awards
Award of Merit

JCC in Manhattan, Samuel Priest Rose Building, New York
American Institute of Architects
New York Chapter Design Awards
Award of Merit

Bahen Centre for Information Technology, University of Toronto
Building Magazine
Outside the Box Award - Urban Design
Honourable Mention

www.dsai.ca
Ontario Association of Architecture
Ideas and Presentation Award

University of Guelph - Humber Building, Toronto
Royal Architectural Institute of Canada - Award of
Excellence for Innovation in Architecture

University of Ontario Institute of Technology, Oshawa
Royal Architectural Institute of Canada - Award of
Excellence for Innovation in Architecture

Diamond and Schmitt Architects
Canada's 50 Best Managed Companies
Deloitte, CIBC, Queen's School of Business

Life Sciences Building, University of British Columbia
Building Owners & Managers Association
The Earth Award for Excellence in environmental
and energy design

The Energy and Environmental Design Award
Special Citation

The Brick Industry Association
Brick in Architecture Award - Institutional

2004

Malton Community Centre, Mississauga
Mississauga Urban Design Award
Award of Excellence

Israeli Foreign Ministry, Jerusalem
The American Institute of Architects
Business Week / Architectural Record Award

Max M. Fisher Music Center, Detroit
Illuminating Engineering Society of North
America - Special Citation

Bahen Centre for Information Technology, University of Toronto
Ontario Consulting Engineering Awards - Award
of Excellence

Environmental Design and Construction Awards
Honorable Mention

Four Seasons Centre for the Performing Arts , Toronto
American Society of Architectural Illustrators
Award of Excellence

Gerstein Science Information Centre, University of Toronto
The Ontario Library Association
Award of Excellence

Ontario Association of Architects
Architectural Excellence Award

Apotex Centre, Jewish Home for the Aged, Baycrest Centre, Toronto
Ontario Association of Architects
Architectural Excellence Award

Diamond and Schmitt Architects
Entrepreneurial Practice Award
Ontario Association of Architects

2003

Cawthra Community Centre, Mississauga
Wood Works Awards
Wood Design Institutional Award

Diamond and Schmitt Architects
The Royal Architectural Institute of Canada
Architectural Firm of the Year

Bahen Centre for Information Technology, University of Toronto
City of Toronto
Architecture and Urban Design Award
Award of Excellence

Ontario Association of Architects
Architectural Excellence Award

Ontario Concrete Awards
Architectural Merit
Precast and Cast-in-place Concrete

Illuminating Engineering Society
Sectional and Regional Illumination Design
Award

National Post Design Exchange Awards
Environmental Category - Bronze

2002

Ways Lane Residence, Toronto
Architecture Magazine / Metropolitan Home
Home of the Year

Lash Miller Chemistry Laboratory, University of Toronto
Ontario Association of Architects
Architectural Excellence - Honourable Mention

2001

The Israeli Ministry of Foreign Affairs, Jerusalem
Royal Architectural Institute of Canada
Excellence in Innovation in Architecture
Building Envelope Innovation

A.J. Diamond
Royal Architectural Institute of Canada Gold
Medal

Cardinal Carter Wing, St. Michael's Hospital, Toronto
Canadian Institute of Steel Construction
Ontario Steel Design Award
Honourable Mention

Marion McCain Arts and Social Sciences Building, Dalhousie University, Halifax
Lieutenant Governor's Award for Architecture
Medal of Excellence

Sweet Pond Residence, Lunenburg
Lieutenant Governor's Award for Architecture
Citation

Ways Lane Residence, Toronto
Toronto Architecture and Urban Design Award of
Excellence

2000

The JCC In Manhattan, New York
Canadian Architect Magazine
Award of Excellence

Cawthra Community Centre, Mississauga
Mississauga Urban Design Awards
Award of Merit for Architectural Innovation

City of Kitchener Urban Design Guidelines
Ontario Professional Planners Institute
Excellence in Planning Award

Apotex Centre Jewish Home for the Aged, Baycrest Centre, Toronto
Canadian Institute of Steel Construction
Ontario Steel Design Awards - Architectural

Ways Lane Residence, Toronto
Ontario Association of Architects
Award of Excellence

Memorial Pool and Health Club, Toronto
Ontario Association of Architects
Award of Excellence

Regent Park Community Health Centre, Toronto
Ontario Association of Architects
Award of Excellence

1999
Capital Information Centre, Ottawa
Ontario Association of Architects
Award of Excellence

Plachta Award for Architectural Excellence

Cornwall Public Library, Cornwall
Ontario Library Association, Library Building
Award for Additions and Alterations to an Existing
Building

Oakwood Village Library and Arts Centre, Toronto
Ontario Library Association
Library Building Award - Urban Neighbourhood

1998
Capital Information Centre, Ottawa
Ottawa Architectural Conservation Award

1997
Capital Information Centre, Ottawa
BOMA Award for Office Efficiency Through
Renovation
Technology in Government Service Renewal
Silver Medal

1996
Student Centre, York University, Toronto
Governor General's Medal

IBM Headquarters, Markham
Ontario Association of Architects
Ideas and Presentations Award

Agnes Etherington Arts Centre, Queen's University, Kingston
Ontario Association of Architects
Ideas and Presentations Award - Honourable
Mention

1995
Earth Sciences Centre, University of Toronto
City of Toronto Urban Design Award

Richmond Hill Central Library, Richmond Hill
Financial Post Design Effectiveness Award

1994
Richmond Hill Central Library, Richmond Hill
Governor General's Medal

Earth Sciences Centre, University of Toronto
Governor General's Medal

Jerusalem City Hall, Jerusalem
American Society of Architectural Perspectivists
Award of Excellence in the Graphic Presentation
of Architecture

1992
Student Centre, York University, Toronto
Architectural Record Magazine/PCA North
American Concrete Building Award of Excellence

Toronto Society of Architects/Toronto Masonry
Awards
Large Project Award

1991
Richmond Hill Central Library, Richmond Hill; Queen's University Library, Kingston; Jerusalem City Hall, Jerusalem; Lois Hancey Aquatic Centre, Toronto
First Prize (Computer Graphics)
ARRIS Design Centre

Newcastle Town Hall, Newcastle
Ontario Association of Architects
Award of Excellence

Burns Hall Officers' Training Facility, Toronto
North York Urban Design Award

1990
Jerusalem City Hall, Jerusalem
Canadian Architect Magazine
Award of Excellence

Earth Sciences Centre, University of Toronto
Toronto Historical Board
Award of Merit

1989
National Ballet School, Toronto
Toronto Historical Board
Award of Merit

Student Centre, York University, Toronto
Canadian Architect Awards
Award of Excellence

1988
Olympic Arch 1988 Calgary Olympics
Olympic Arts Festival Gold Medal

1987
Metropolitan Toronto Central YMCA
Ontario Association of Architects
Award of Excellence

Burns Building, Calgary
Credit Foncier Award

1986
Metropolitan Toronto Central YMCA
Governor General's Medal

Citadel Theatre, Edmonton
Governor General's Medal

1985
Village Terrace, Toronto
Governor General's Medal

Canadian Housing Design Council Award

1984
Japanese Restaurant Centre
Canadian Architect Magazine
Award of Excellence

Royal Opera House Covent Garden, UK
International Competition Finalist

Berkeley Castle, Toronto
National Award of Honour
Heritage Canada Foundation

1983
St. Michael's Lands, Toronto
Ontario Association of Architects
Toronto Life Homes Residential Award -High Rise
Multiple Housing

Berkeley Castle, Toronto
Credit Foncier Award
Honourable Mention

La Tete Defence, Paris
International Design Competition
Honourable Mention

Village Terrace, Toronto
Ontario Association of Architects
Residential Award - High Rise

1982
Alcan Aluminum Corporation, Toronto
Interiors Magazine Award
Executive Office Winner

Metropolitan Toronto Central YMCA
Canadian Architect Magazine
Award of Excellence

1979
Heritage Canada Communications Award

1978
Citadel Theatre, Edmonton
Stelco Design Award

City of Edmonton Design Award

Westover Park Estates, St. Mary's, Ontario
Canadian Architect Yearbook
Award of Excellence

Dundas Sherbourne Housing, Toronto
Canadian Housing Design, Council Award

Urban Design Magazine Award

Habitation Space International Award

1977
Queen's University Housing, Kingston
Heritage Canada Regional Award of Honour

Talka Community, Mississauga
Canadian Architect Magazine
Award of Excellence

1976
Dundas Sherbourne Housing, Toronto
City of Toronto Non-Profit Housing Corporation
Design Award

Hydro Block, Toronto
City of Toronto Non-Profit Housing Corporation
Design Award

Urban Design Magazine, New York
Design Award

1975
Housing Union Building, University of Alberta
Award for Residential Design - Honourable
Mention

1971
Alcan Executive Offices, Toronto
Ontario Association of Architects
Award of Excellence

1969
York Square, Toronto
Ontario Association of Architects
Award of Excellence

Habitation Space International Award

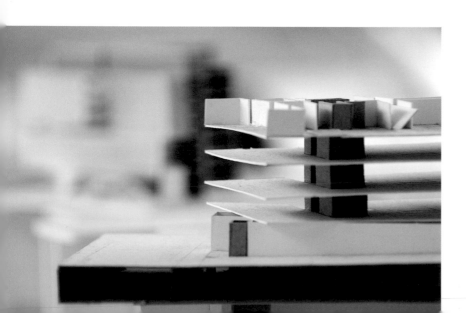

WRITINGS BY A.J. DIAMOND

1963. "Participants-Eye Views i: Seminar at Cranbrook Journal of Architectural Education 18(3), December: 38-39.

1965-70. Architecture Canada (Royal Architectural Institute of Canada). (Associate/Contributing Editor during these years).

1966. "Universities, Introduction." Architecture Canada 43(10), October: 43.

1967. "The New City." Habitat 10(1), January/February: 33-35.

1967. "Expo 67." AM Journal (American Institute of Architects) 47(2), February: 42-56.

1967. "Expo and the Future City." Parallel 1(6), February/March: 32-36.

1968. "A Plea for Performance Standards." AIA Journal (American Institute of Architects) 50(1), July: 54-55.

1969. "Design Priorities Questioned." Architecture Canada (9), September: 14.

1971. "Two Aspects of Services — Quality and Economy." Canadian Building, September: 28.

1972. "Density, Distribution and Costs." Research paper for Central Mortgage and Housing Corporation,

1974. "Town Building or Town Planning?" Canadian Architect 19(1), January: 35-36.

1976. "Residential Density and Housing Form." Journal of Architectural Education 29(3), February: 15-16.

1978. "On Sleeping with An Elephant; Canada and America." Process: Architecture 5: 26-29.

1978. "P.O.V.: What This Country Needs Is a Good Provincial Architecture." Toronto Life, May: 190.

1978. "A Sense of Place." Canadian Forum 58(681): June/July: 10-11.

1978/79. "Drawings." Descant 9(3) & 10(1): 26, 38, 48, 56, 67, 74, 95, 110.

1979. "Rehabilitation in Practice." In Rehabilitation of Buildings: Proceedings (Second Canadian Building Congress, Toronto, Ontario. October 15-17, 1979). Ottawa: National Research Council of Canada. Pages 15-22.

1981. "Renovation Design." LCN Newsletter, April: 1-4.

1982. "A Critique of the Planning and Building Design of Winnipeg." In The Winter City (Conference sponsored by the Canadian Housing Design Council in co-operation with the Continuing Education Division, the University of Manitoba, Winter 1982). Winnipeg: Canadian Housing Design Council. Pages 3-8.

1992. "Staying in Shape." Toronto Life, November: 56-59.

1995. "Die Kosten trägt die Allgemeinheit: Über Einkaufszentren auf der grünen Wiese." planen + bauen, June: 27.

1996. Golden, Anne; Diamond, Jack; McCormack, Thomas; Prichard, Robert; Wong, Joseph. "Greater Toronto" Report of the GTA Task Force. January

1997. "Tree House." Writing Home: A PEN Canada Anthology. Edited by Constance Rook. Toronto: McClelland and Stewart: 29-33

1997. "A.J. (Jack) Diamond." Everybody's Favourites: Canadians talk about books that changed their lives. Edited by Arlene Perly Rae. Toronto: The Penguin Group: 31-32.

2003. "New Deal for Cities Critical." The Globe and Mail, December 3.

2004. "City of Dreams", The Globe and Mail, December 12.

2006. "Our Sickly Suburbs: We have the cure. Where is the courage?" The Globe and Mail, August 5.

2007. "Urban Form, Transportation and Sustainability." Ideas that Matter, July 30.

2007. "Sprawl is our 'Inconvenient Truth'." The Globe and Mail, May 18.

WRITINGS BY DONALD SCHMITT

1980. "Urban Consolidation and Infill." LCN Newsletter, June: 1-4.

1987. "Western Section - Bathurst Street to Humber River." In A Charette in the City: The Gardiner Expressway (O.A.A. Convention, Toronto, March 4-6, 1987). Toronto: Ontario Association of Architects. Pages 29-43.

1987. "O.A.A. Charette, A Report: Team Three, Western Section." Canadian Architect 321(7), July: 36-37.

1987. "Consensus and Other Concerns." Canadian Architect 32(7), September: 18-33. (Editor).

1990. Housing on Toronto's Main Streets: A Design Competition: Conditions and Programme. Toronto: City of Toronto.

1993. "Case Studies: Critique." In Public Art Symposium: Report of the Proceedings (Mayor's Symposium on Public Art, Hamilton, Ontario, May 30, 1992). Edited by Cheryl York. Hamilton: Department of Culture and Recreation, City of Hamilton: 31-39.

ABOUT THE FIRM, SIGNIFICANT PROJECTS AND CONTEMPORARY ARCHITECTURAL ISSUES

1968. Mitchell, Harris. "Small Change, Big Improvement." Canadian Homes, August: 6-9.

1972. "A.J. Diamond and Barton Myers: 15 Works." a + u (Architecture & Urbanism) 2(5), May: 15-63.

1973. "Cities: the Low-rise Alternative." Time, 16 April: 14-16.

1975. Kuwabara, Bruce and Barry Sampson. "Diamond and Myers: The Form of Reform/Great Canadian Architects and Planners 3." City Magazine 1(5/6), August/September: 29-47.

1978. Jackson, Anthony. The Democratization of Canadian Architecture (Library of Canadian Architecture). Halifax: Tech-Press.

1979. Littman, Sol. "Jack Diamond's Architecture Has Changed Toronto's Face." Toronto Star, 4 March.

1979. McKelvey, Merilyn. "Main Street and Heritage Conservation." LCN Newsletter, October: 1-6.

1981. Bernstein, William and Ruth Cawker. Contemporary Canadian Architecture: The Mainstream and Beyond. Don Mills, Ontario: Fitzhenry and Whiteside.

1981. Cawker, Ruth and William Bernstein (Compilers). Building with Words: Canadian Architects on Architecture. Toronto: Coach House Press.

1981. Garland, Kevin and Paul Syme. "Conversion and Renovation for Residential Use." LCN Newsletter, November: 1-6.

1982. Royle, John C. "Sprawl, the Curse of North America." Community Ontario 26(2), March/April: 12-13.

1982. "Perspective: Renewal." Canadian Architect 27(9), September: 4.

1983. "From Mies to Metaphors." Canadian Architect 28(5), May: 23-38.

1984. Boone, Ned. "The Box Rebellion." Homes (Toronto Life), Spring: 1-147-48.

1985. McBride, Eve. "The New Y: A User's Report." Toronto Life, January: 14.

1985. "A Toronto: La Nuova Sede YMCA." Abitare (233), April: 92-95.

1985. Richards, Larry. "Making a Dignified Place: The Metropolitan Central YMCA, Toronto." Canadian Architect 30(4), April: 24-34.

1985. Richardson, Jeff. "Controversial YMCA Highly Functional." Canadian Building, June: 51-53.

1985. "New Products from Old Mills." Progressive Architecture 66(11), November: 94-99.

1986. Boddy, Trevor. "Making/Breaking the Canadian Street." In Metropolitan Mutations: The Architecture of Emerging Public Spaces (R.A.I.C. Annual; l). Edited by Detlef Mertins. Toronto: Little, Brown and Company (Canada) Limited. Pages 167-78 and pages 175-76.

1986. Renault, Odile. "A Sampling of the Nation's Far-flung Works of Quality." Architecture 75(9), September: 68-71.

1987. Cawker, Ruth (Editor). Toronto: Le Nouveau, Nouveau Monde: Contemporary Architecture of Toronto. Toronto: Government of Ontario. Pages 28-29.

1987. Boddy, Trevor. "The Bush League: Four Approaches to Regionalism in Recent Canadian Architecture." Center: A Journal for Architecture in America 3: 100-107.

1987. Robinson, John. "Donald Schmitt: Architecture for People." Toronto Star, April 26.

1987. Lasker, David. "The Charette." Perspectives (The Newsletter of the Ontario Association of Architects) 1(1), July: 2-5.

1987. Lasker, David. "An Award-winning Project of Well-Defined Spaces and Exposed Structural Elements. Canadian Interiors 24(12), December: 38-41.

1988. Cawker, Ruth and William Bernstein. Contemporary Canadian Architecture: The Mainstream and Beyond. Revised and Expanded Edition. Markham, Ontario: Fitzhenry and Whiteside.

1990. Falconer, Tim. "Diamond Mined." Toronto Life, March: 90-96.

1990. Arcidi, Philip. "Inquiry: Campus Infill." Progressive Architecture 71(4), April: 100, 107. 1990. Bisi, Lucia. "Il Centro di Scienze Naturali di Toronto." L'ARCA 37, April: 26-33.

1990. Boddy, Trevor. "Building Appraisal: Earth Sciences Centre, University of Toronto." Canadian Architect 35(5), May: 28-35.

1990. "Jerusalem City Hall Square." Canadian Architect 35(7), July: 18-23.

1990. Carter, Brian. "Town and Gown." Architects' Journal 192(6), 8 August: 28-33.

1991. "Housing on Toronto's Main Streets". Places: A Quarterly Journal of Environmental Design 7(2), Winter: 48-76.

1991. "Urban Ecology: Earth Sciences Centre." Architectural Record 179(2), February: 108-109.

1991. Evans, Craig. "Global Landscape: East Meets West." Landscape Architecture 81(8), August: 40.

1992. Crinion, Elizabeth. "The Right Angles." Canadian House and Home 14(1), February/March: 48-53. 1992. Rybczynski, Witold. "Diamond's Style Forever." Globe and Mail, 9 June: Dio.

1992. Callwood's National Treasures: Jack Diamond (Interview with June Callwood, May 20, 1992). Toronto: Produced by Contact Communications for VISION TV. Videotape.

1992. Mertins, Detlef. "Redefining the Spaces of Modernity." Canadian Architect 37(5), May: 15-23.

1992. Rochon, Lisa. "Human Designs." International Contract, June/July: 3 pages.

1993. Adrienne Clarkson Presents: A.J. Diamond – Architect. Toronto: Canadian Broadcasting Corporation. Videotape.

1993. Ferrara, Luigi. "Going Global: Ontario Architects Take the Leap." Perspectives (The Journal of the Ontario Association of Architects) 1(1), Spring: 8-13.

1993. Carter, Brian. "Campus Showpiece." Architectural Review 193(1155), May: 24-29.

1993. Kroyanker, David. The Making of City Hall Complex, Jerusalem. Jerusalem: Ariel Publishing House.

1993. Martin, Patrick. "Diamond Creates New Jewel." Globe and Mail, 28 June: CI.

1994. Emanuel, Muriel (Editor). Contemporary Architects. 3rd Edition. New York: St. Martin's Press. 1994. Kalman, Harold. A History of Canadian Architecture: Volume 2. Toronto: Oxford University Press.

1994. Graham, Owen (Editor). Architecture Canada: The Governor General's Awards for Architecture, 1994. Ottawa: Canada Council and The Royal Architectural Institute of Canada: 118-124 and 150-57.

1994. Kroyanker, David. Jerusalem Architecture. New York: Vendrome Press.

1994. Richards, Larry Wayne. "Temple on the Fringe." Canadian Architect 39(2), February: 14-23.

1994 Gzowski, Peter. "Windows and Rooms: Peter Gzowski Interviews A.J. Diamond." Brick (48), Spring: 46-58.

1995. Warson, Albert. "Altered States: Canada." World Architecture (37): 65-67.

1995. Kroyanker, David. "The New Design Code of Jerusalem: The Fashion of Quoting." AI: Architecture of Israel (21), April: 4-5, 16-17.

1995. "A Tale of Two Cities." Progressive Architecture (5), May: 38-39.

1995. Carter, Brian. "Canadian Civitas." Architectural Review 197(1179), May: 68-73.

1995. Turner, Michael. "Work Abroad I: New Civic Foundations." Canadian Architect 40(6), June: 16-21.

1995. Soloman, Nancy B. "Wiring the Library." Architecture 10 October: 118-119.

1998. Goldstein, Bonnie and Shulman, Jaclyn, editors. "Building Jerusalem's City Hall." Voices from the Heart, Toronto: McClelland and Stewart: 216-218

1999. de Beer, Piet. "Diamond in Canada." South Africa Architect, September/October

2001. Polo, Marco. "Commitment, Service, Dialogue." RAIC Gold Medal 2001

2002. "Alumbrera." 100 of the World's Best Houses, Australia: Images Publishing: 16-17

2003. "Marion McCain Arts and Sciences Building." Educational Spaces, Australia: Images Publishing: 152-155

2003. Polo, Marco. "Green Giant." Canadian Architect, January

2003. Drucker, Stephen. "An Outside Influence – Blurring the Lines Between Indoors and out on Mustique." Architectural Digest, March 116-123

2003. Wickens, Steven. "Diamond Backs Smart Growth." The Globe and Mail, April 4.

2003. Levin, Michael. "Jerusalem of Gold." Canadian Architect, May.

2003. Levin, Michael & Czarnecki, John E. "Diamond and Schmitt integrate a sublime onyx jewel box into the highly secure Israeli Foreign Ministry." Architectural Record, June.

2003. Barreneche, Raul. "Metropolitan Home Architecture." Metropolitan Home, July.

2003. Bentley-Mays, John. "Commanding Performance." Canadian

Architect, September: 21-78

2003. Kinzer, Stephen. "Concerto for Orchestra and Hopeful City." The New York Times, September

2003. Fishlinsky, Sandra. "Jack Diamond – a passion for building." Lifestyles Magazine, September.

2003. "Israeli Ministry of Foreign Affairs, Jerusalem." Detail, November

2004. "Sweet Pond." Objekt, Spring: 104-109

2004. Marchese, Ines. "An Interview with Jack Diamond." Perspectives, April

2004. Schwatz, Martin. "Detroit: Catalytic Conversion." Architecture, April

2004. Stohr, Kate. "Redevelopment Plans Have Long Failed in Detroit. The Newest Round Are Different, but Will They Work?" Architectural Record, August

2004. Jen, Lesie. "Life in the Fast Lane." Canadian Architect, October.

2005. "Infill Housing, une philosophie durable." Interieurs 32, January.

2005. Chodikoff, Ian. "Casting Light." Canadian Architect, January .

2005. Rochon, Lisa. "Can our city be beautiful in the next five years?" The Globe and Mail, February 7.

2005. Marchese, Ines. "Urban Issues and Politics: A Discussion with Jack Diamond." Perspectives, April.

2005. McKenzie-Glavez, Kim. "Leitmotif." Canadian Interiors, June

2005. McGreal, Ryan. "Designing Livable Cities: An Interview with Donald Schmitt." Raise the Hammer, November 28.

2005. Scott, Sarah. "All Ears." Azure, November/December: 54 - 57

2005. Sobchak, Peter. "Limited Means as a Catalyst for Innovation." Building Magazine, December

2006. Sidimus, Joysanne and Anderson, Carol. "Jack Diamond." Reflections in a Dancing Eye: Investigating the Artists Role in Canadian Society: 116 - 123

2006. Webster, Paul, "Sounds of Silence." Canadian Geographic, January/February: 56 - 62

2006. Amiel, Barbara. "Bravissimo!" Maclean's, June: 61 – 64

2006. Ashenburg, Katherine. "The House that Jack Built." Toronto Life, July: 64 – 70

2006. "The Esplanade infuses arts into the heart of a community." ArchitecturalRecord.com, August.

2006. King, Andrew. "Hat Trick." Canadian Architect, September: 32 - 37

2006. Richards, Larry Wayne. "Sight and Sound." Azure, September

2006. Tommasini, Anthony. "A Brand New 'Ring' in a Brand New Space." The New York Times, September 14.

2006. Porter, Andrew. "New Gloss in a Glass House." The Times Literary Supplement, October 6

2006. "New Order of the Garter." Irish Times, November 4.

2006. Schnieder, Jay W. "Green Goes Underground." Building Design and Construction, November: 59-61

2007. "2007 Top 100 Architecture Firms." 2007 BD World Architecture 100, January

2007. Blanthorn, Jon Scott. "Cultural Transparency." InDesign, May

2007. Kieran, Christopher. "Four Seasons Centre for the Performing Arts – Citation for Excellence." ArchitecturalRecord.com, August

2007. Harris, Paul. Shakespeare Theatre Buiding Up, Company's New Space Elevates Profile." Variety, September 28

2007. Dietsch, Deborah K. "Modernism's March on Washington." Wasington Times, September

2007. Marks, Peter. "A Bold New Stage for DC." Washington Post, September

2007. Crabb, Michael. "Capitol Idea." Auditoria, October: 34 - 39

2007. " Intellectual and Artistic Renaissance." The Economist, October 10

2007. Allderdice, Jacob. "Campus Ideals." Canadian Architect, November

2007. Crabb, Michael. "Level Headed: Jack Diamond's ability to balance beauty and utility has made him the international arts community's go-to man." The National Post, November 3.

2007. Murphy, Lisa. "Canadian Stylemakers." Canadian House and Home, December: 166

2007. Steiner, David. "One with Nature." Azure, December

2007. Bozikovic, Alex. "Toronto Public Housing Gets Green Makeover." Architectural Record, December

2007. Isherwood. Charles. "Shakespeare's New House Makes Room for Marlowe." The New York Times, November 15.

2007. Kennicott, Philip. "Shakespeare and the City, at a New Stage." The Washington Post, November 18.

2008. "Sidney Harman Hall - Harman Center for the Arts." ArchitecturalRecord.com, January.

2008. "The Big List: World's largest practices." BD 2008 World Architecture 100, January

INDEX

Academic Library / University of Ontario Institute of Technology, Oshawa *150*, 286-293, 328-329

Addison, Joseph 102

adobe housing 233, *235*

aesthetics, with plan order 98-103

Agnes Etherington Art Centre / Queen's University, Kingston 274-275, 322

Allston Campus, Harvard University65

Alumbrera House, Mustique 126-129, 322

Anthony P. Toldo Health Education Centre / University of Windsor 302-303, 322

Apotex Centre, Toronto 162-165, 322

arts, architecture for the 252-255

AT&T Building, New York 12

Bahen Centre for Information Technology / University of Toronto 26, *125*, *150*, *236*, 310-319, 322

Banff Centre Campus Master Plan 56-59, 322

Bank Street Building Competition, Parliament Hill, Ottawa 38-41, 322-323

Bank Street Senate Office Building *185*

Barcelona Pavilion 99

Bastille Opera, Paris 253

Berkeley Castle, Toronto *218*, 226-227, 323

Bernini, Gianlorenzo 25, 123

Berton Library. See Pierre Berton Resource Library

Betty Oliphant Theatre / Canada's National Ballet School, Toronto 26, 220-221, 323

Beverley Place, Toronto 80-81

Bibliothèque nationale de France 101

bio-filter walls 21, 74, *117*, 184-185, 196, *199*, 201

Black Star Collection 304

bore hole technology 184, 189
Borehole Thermal Energy Storage System (BTESS) 189

Bowling Alone: The Collapse and Revival of American Communities by Robert Putnam 26-27

Bradshaw Amphitheatre. See Four Seasons

Centre for the Performing Arts

Brick Works. See Evergreen at the Brick Works

Brunelleschi, Filippo 233

Burns Building, Calgary 216, *217*

Calgary Centre for the Performing Arts 216

Callas, Maria 254

Cambridge City Hall 116-117, 323

Campus Master Plan / McGill University, Montreal 300-301, 323

Canadian Chancery, Prague 224-225, 323

Canadian Opera Company 253

Capital Information Centre, Ottawa 222-223, 323

Carcassonne, France 79

Cawthra Community Centre, Mississauga 242-245, 323

Centre for Advanced Manufacturing and Design Technologies / Sheridan College, Brampton 202-205, 323

Centre Pompidou, Paris 26

Charlie Condominiums, Toronto 94, 323

College Residences, Lakeshore Campus and North Campus, Humber College, Toronto 138-141, 323-324

Colucci, Gregory (Diamond and Schmitt Architects) 334

Computer Science and Engineering Building / University of Michigan, Ann Arbor *103*, *285*, 294-299, 324

conservation. See environmental issues

context, architectural 24-29

Country Day School Performing Arts Centre, King City 278-279, 324

Covent Garden, London *254*

Dalhousie University: Marion McCain Faculty of Arts and Sciences Building 36-37, 326

Davenport Wing, Lash Miller Chemistry Building / University of Toronto 248-249, 324

Davidson, Martin (Diamond and Schmitt Architects) 334

Detroit Symphony 255

Diamond, A.J. (Diamond and Schmitt Architects) 9, 332

Diamond and Schmitt Architects 11-22, 227 Awards 338-340; Bibliography 341-343; Firm 331; Partners 332-333; Principals 11-22, 334-337
Projects: See Academic Library, UOIT; Agnes Etherington Art Centre; Alumbrera House; Anthony P. Toldo Health Education Centre, Windsor; Apotex Centre; Bahen Centre for Information Technology, Toronto; Banff Centre Campus Master Plan and Implementation; Bank Street Building Competition; Berkeley Castle; Betty Oliphant Theatre; Cambridge City Hall; Campus Master Plan, McGill; Canadian Chancery; Capital Information Centre; Cawthra Community Centre; Charlie Condominiums; College Residences, Lakeshore Campus and North Campus, Humber; Computer Science and Engineering Building, Michigan; Country Day School Performing Arts Centre; Centre for Advanced Manufacturing and Design Technologies, Sheridan; Davenport Wing, Lash Miller Building, Toronto; Earth Sciences Centre, Toronto; East Bayfront Master Plan Proposal; Esplanade Arts and Heritage Centre; Evergreen at the Brick Works; Four Seasons Centre for the Performing Arts; Garter Lane Arts Centre; Gerstein Science Information Centre, Toronto; Holy Blossom Temple; Hudson Condominiums; Indigo Residence; Integrated Sciences Building, Drexel; Israeli Ministry of Foreign Affairs; Jewish Community Center in Manhattan; Jerusalem City Hall; Leggatt Hall and Watts Hall, Queen's; Legislative Assembly of Ontario, Renovation Master Plan and Implementation; Li Ka Shing Knowledge Institute; Life Sciences Centre, UBC; Life Sciences Complex, McGill; Los Alamos Civic Center; Maria Shchuka District Branch Library; Marian McCain Faculty of Arts and Sciences Building, Dalhousie; Max M. Fisher Music Center; Medical Education Building, Windsor; Memorial Pool; Metro Central YMCA; Minto Lonsdale Condominiums; New Brunswick Museum; Ontario Science Centre Master Plan and Renovations; Pierre Berton Resource Library; Regent Park Community Health Centre; Richmond Hill Central Library; School of Computer Science and Engineering, Hebrew University; School of Image Arts; Sidney Harman Hall; Southbrook Vineyards; Student Centre, York; Susur Restaurant; TEDCO's Corus Building; Thayer Building, Michigan; University of Guelph-Humber; University of Ontario Institute of Technology, Campus and Buildings; Urban Block Redevelopment, Regent Park; Ways Lane Project list 322-329; Staff 330

Disney Hall, Los Angeles 25

Don Jail, Toronto 122

Dow, David (Diamond and Schmitt Architects) 334

Drexel University: Integrated Sciences Building 112-115, 325

Duomo di Siena 124

Earth Sciences Centre / University of Toronto 29, 306-307, 324

East Bayfront Master Plan Proposal, Toronto 66-67, 324

economy of means 232-237

education, architecture for 280-284

elements of architecture 120-125

ENIAC (Electronic Numerical Integrator and Computer) 298

environmental and conservation issues 182-187, 232-237

EPCOR Centre for the Performing Arts, Calgary 217

Esplanade Arts and Heritage Centre, Medicine Hat 104-107, 324

Etherington Art Centre. See Agnes Etherington Art Centre

Evergreen at the Brick Works, Toronto 200-201, 324

Fisher Center. See Max M. Fisher Music Center

Florida, Richard 9

Four Seasons Centre for the Performing Arts, Toronto 253-254, 256-265, 324

Garden City movement 77

Garnier, Charles 254

Garter Lane Arts Centre, Waterford 266-267, 325

Gaudi, Antoni 25, 26, 27

Gehry, Frank 25

geodesic dome 236

geothermal heating 184

Gerstein Science Information Centre Master Plan and Renovations / University of Toronto 48-55, 325

Graham, Robert (Diamond and Schmitt Architects) 335

Guggenheim Museum, New York 25, 151

Ken Greenberg and Associates 74-75

Harman Hall. See Sidney Harman Hall

Harvard University 65

Haussmann, Baron (Georges-Eugène) 26, 61

Hebrew University of Jerusalem: School of Computer Science and Engineering 308-309

Holy Blossom Temple, Toronto 178-179, 325

Hudson Condominiums, Toronto 90-91, 325

Humber College: Residences, Lakeshore and North Campuses 138-141, 323-324

illumination and movement 148-151

Image Arts. See School of Image Arts

Indigo Residence, Mustique 212-213, 325

inner order in design 98-103

Integrated Sciences Building / Drexel University, Philadelphia 112-115, 325

Israeli Ministry of Foreign Affairs, Jerusalem 123, 152-161, 325

Jacobs, Jane 218

Jefferson, Thomas 281

Jerusalem City Hall 26, 30-35, 149, 325

Jewish Community Center in Manhattan 42-47, 325

Johnson, Philip 12

Jugendstil Building, Prague 224

Kabriel, Helen (Diamond and Schmitt Architects) 335

Kahn, Louis 99

Kyoto Accord 184

Lakeshore Campus Residence. See College Residences, Lakeshore Campus and North Campus / Humber College

Lash Miller Chemistry Building. See Davenport Wing, Lash Miller Chemistry Building

Leadership in Energy and Environmental Design 237; LEED Gold certification 74, 95, 117, 146; LEED Platinum certification 201

Leckman, Michael (Diamond and Schmitt Architects) 335

Leggatt Hall and Watts Hall / Queen's University, Kingston 130-133, 325-326

Legislative Assembly of Ontario Renovation Master Plan and Implementation, Toronto 228-231, 326

L'Enfant, Pierre 61

Le Thoronet Abbey, France 100

Levitt, William 77

Levittown 77, 78

Li Ka Shing Knowledge Institute / St. Michael's Hospital, Toronto 88-89, 326

Life Sciences Centre / University of British Columbia, Vancouver 206-211, 326

Life Sciences Complex / McGill University, Montreal 96-97, 326

Los Alamos Civic Center 70-73, 326

Maria Shchuka District Branch Library, Toronto 142-143, 326

Marion McCain Faculty of Arts and Social Sciences Building / Dalhousie University, Halifax 36-37, 326-327

Markson Borooah Hodgson Architects 74-75

Max M. Fisher Music Center, Detroit 268-273, 326

McCain Building. See Marion McCain Faculty of Arts and Social Sciences Building

McCluskie, Gary (Diamond and Schmitt Architects) 336

McGill University: Campus Master Plan 300-301; Life Sciences Complex 96-97

Medical Education Building / University of Windsor 146-147, 327

Meier, Richard 253

Memorial Pool, Toronto 246-247, 327

Metro Central YMCA, Toronto 134-137, 327

Mies van der Rohe 20, 99, 234

Minto Lonsdale Condominiums, Toronto 95, 327

Modernism 18, 99, 234

Mustique. See Alumbrera House; Indigo Residence

Nash, John 125

National Ballet School. See Betty Oliphant Theatre, Canada's National Ballet School

New Brunswick Museum, Saint John 276-277, 327

North Campus Residence. See College Residences, Lakeshore Campus and North Campus / Humber College

Northland Shopping Center, Detroit 80

Notre Dame, Paris 121

Oliphant Theatre. See Betty Oliphant Theatre, Canada's National Ballet School
Olympic Stadium, Beijing 14

Olympic Stadium, Montreal 233

Ontario Science Centre Master Plan and Renovations, Toronto 172-177, 327

Ontario Science Centre, Great Hall 219

Ott, Carlos 253

Paris Opera 254

Pei, I.M. 18

Perrault, Dominique 101

Peter the Great 124

Piano, Renzo 14, 20, 26

Piazza di Spagna 124

Pierre Berton Resource Library, Vaughan 166-171, 327

Potemkin Stairs, Odessa 151

Pratt, Thom (Diamond and Schmitt Architects) 336

Pythagoras 125

Queen's University: Agnes Etherington Art Centre 274-275, 322; Leggatt Hall and Watts Hall 130-133, 326

Regent Park, Toronto, Ontario 63-64, 74-75, 238-241

Regent Park Community Health Centre, Toronto 238-241, 327

renovation and reuse of old structures 214-218

Richard Bradshaw Amphitheatre. See Four Seasons Centre for the Performing Arts, Toronto

Richmond Hill Central Library, Richmond Hill 108-111, 327

Rockefeller Plaza, New York 63

Rogers, Richard 26

Royal Ontario Museum, Toronto 237

Royal Opera House, Covent Garden, London 254

Rybczynski, Witold 11-22

Ryerson University: School of Image Arts 304-305

St. James Town, Toronto 80, 81

St. Michael's Hospital, Toronto. See Li Ka Shing Knowledge Institute

St. Peter's Basilica, Rome 12, 123

Saarinen, Eero 294

Salk Institute, La Jolla 99

Santa Maria del Fiore cathedral, Florence 233

Scala Regia 123

Scarborough, Ontario 77-78

Schmitt, Donald (Diamond and Schmitt Architects) 9, 333

School of Computer Science and Engineering/ The Hebrew University of Jerusalem 308-309, 327

School of Image Arts / Ryerson University, Toronto 304-305, 328

Shakespeare Theater Company, Washington 83

Shchuka Library. See Maria Shchuka District Branch Library

Sheridan College: Centre for Advanced Manufacturing and Deign Technologies 202-205, 323

Siber, Birgit (Diamond and Schmitt Architects) 336

Sidney Harman Hall, Washington 82-87, 328

Soules, Jon (Diamond and Schmitt Architects) 337

Southbrook Vineyards, Niagara-on-the-Lake 144-145, 328

Sports Palace, Berlin 26

Stockhausen, Karlheinz 19

Student Centre / York University, Toronto 118-119, 328

sustainable design 182-187

Susur Restaurant, Toronto 180-181, 328

Sydney Opera House 236-237

Michael Szabo (Diamond and Schmitt Architects) 337

Szaszkiewicz, Paul (Diamond and Schmitt Architects) 337

Taillibert, Roger 233

Taj Mahal 151

TEDCO's Corus Building, Toronto 68-69, 328

Temple Mount, Jerusalem *30-31*

Thayer Building / University of Michigan, Ann Arbor 250-251, 328

Toldo Health Centre. See Anthony P. Toldo Health Education Centre

Uffizi Gallery, Florence 151

University College Master Plan; Oxford University *64*

University of British Columbia: Life Sciences Centre 206-211, 326

University of Guelph-Humber, Toronto 21, 196-199, 328-329

University of Ontario Institute of Technology, Oshawa. Academic Library *150*, 286-293; Campus and Buildings *102*, *151*, 184-185, *186*, 188-195, *282*, *283*, 328-329

University of Michigan: Computer Science and Engineering Building *103*, *285*, 294-299, 324; Thayer Building 250-251, 328

University of Toronto: Bahen Centre for Information Technology *125*, *150*, 236, 310-319, 322; Davenport Wing, Lash Miller Chemistry Building 248-249, 324; Earth Sciences Building 306-307, 324; Gerstein Science Information Centre 48-55, 325

University of Virginia 281

University of Windsor: Medical Education Building 146-147, 327; Anthony P. Toldo Health Education Centre 302-303, 322

Urban Block Redevelopment, Regent Park, Toronto 74-75, 329

urban planning, urban density 60-65, 76-81

Utzon, Jørn 236-237

Venturi, Robert 19

Warhol, Andy 25, *28*

Watts Hall. See Leggatt Hall and Watts Hall / Queen's University, Kingston

Ways Lane, Toronto 92-93, 329

Wright, Frank Lloyd 25, 122, 151, 253

York University: Student Centre 118-119, 328

zoning issues 80

IMAGE CREDITS

Every effort has been made to contact copyright holders. In the event of an omission or error, Diamond and Schmitt should be notified at 384 Adelaide St. West, Suite 300, Toronto, Ontario, M5V 1R7

Insight and On Site **was produced by Angel Editions**
under the direction of Sara Angel

Project Managers
Elizabeth Gyde
Nisha Lewis

Book Design
Anita Matusevics
Jason Halter
Wonder inc.

Editors
Patricia Holtz
Rosemary Shipton

Assistant Editor
Amy Hick

Image Production
Jeff Hale
Doug Laxdal
The Gas Company

Health, Health Care
and
Health Economics

1Health Economics in Full Swing

Gerard Sandier
1996